WHAT PEOPLE ARE SAYING ABOUT

DRENCHED

"Jeff Stanford has been my friend for over 30 years. He is a rock-solid family man, friend, pastor, and engaging teacher of the Word of God. I have met very few men who have the revelation and understanding of the Holy Spirit that Jeff does. He communicates that wisdom in written form in a way that speaks to those who are tired of the status quo and ready to experience God's presence at another level. *Drenched* is very appropriate for such a time as this, and I believe it is timely and undoubtedly Spirit-directed. The wisdom, insight, and life-proven principles that are shared in this book will certainly revolutionize your walk with God. I pray that as you read the words in *Drenched*, your life will never be the same!"

—Bishop David Smith
Lead Pastor, Oak Park Church, Mobile, Alabama

"I'm 57 years old and was practically born on a Pentecostal church pew! Pastor Jeff Stanford is one of my top five favorite preachers of all time that I've ever heard in my life. He doesn't follow any of the trends or try to copy anyone else. Just full of the fire of God, and I am excited to read anything that he writes."

—Lawrence Bishop II
Co-Pastor Solid Rock Church, Monroe, Ohio

"Jeff Stanford is a powerful evangelist, compassionate pastor, and accomplished leader. Few people have the spiritual giftedness to fulfill all three of these roles excellently. But that is exactly who he is. His many years as an evangelist laid a firm foundation for a pastoral style that is biblically based and fully open to the moving of the Holy Spirit.

"In *Drenched*, Pastor Stanford clearly explains in everyday vernacular what it means for an individual to live a lifestyle that is saturated by the Holy Spirit of God. This book needs to be not only on the shelf of every pastor's study but also on the coffee table of every believer. Every Christian who sincerely desires to be baptized with the Holy Spirit needs to read this book. Every disciple of the Lord Jesus Christ who has a spiritual hunger to go deeper in God should consume every word written on its pages. Without a doubt, *Drenched* should be considered a primer when it comes to the subject of the fullness of the Holy Spirit in the life of the believer."

—Terry Hart
Alabama Church of God Administrative Bishop

"Bishop Jeff Stanford, through this book *Drenched*, is speaking to us and leading and guiding us to stay in the very presence of God! We will find our purpose in God's presence. We will be equipped in God's presence and given the power and leading of God when we get drenched in the very presence of God."

—Dr. Tommy Combs
Living Word Ministries

"Jeff Stanford, whose ministry I have experienced and whose life I have observed, lives what he has written in *Drenched*. His authentic, personal testimonial bears witness to his genuinely inspiring walk in the Spirit. As you read each chapter, you will discover what it means to live in the Spirit and know the assurance that comes to those who become drenched. As Jeff reveals by the thesis of experiencing the Holy Spirit, you will understand that the message is more than a one-time experience. It is a way of life with continual blessing and strength in the abiding presence of the Holy Spirit."

—Benjamin B. McGlamery
Retired Pastor

"Jeff Stanford is known as a preacher anointed of the Holy Spirit. He is also one of the greatest encouragers I have ever met. This book, *Drenched*, has those qualities intertwined throughout his writings. It will be a great tool to help you walk a victorious life."

—David Jarvis
West Virginia Church of God Administrative Bishop

"Pastor Jeff Stanford shares his journey and experience of the 'drenched life' found only through the fresh revelation and transformative power of the Holy Spirit. Written with vigor, depth, and uncontainable joy, *Drenched: Thoroughly Covered and Completely Filled* is for those new in their faith or those still seeking who do not yet know God. It is simplistic enough to be understood and grasped and written in a way that people can relate to. Yet, at the same time, for those who have been walking with the Lord for quite some time, it is in-depth enough that it challenges us to grow deeper in our relationship with the Holy Spirit, opening our eyes to things we may never have seen. Be prepared to be changed as you become drenched in the Holy Spirit's presence. It will affect your whole life and everything around you."

—Dr. Michael Welborn
Pastor, Pelham Church of God

Cover design by: Sara Young
Cover photo by: Raven Cannon

ISBN: 978-1-962401-09-8   1 2 3 4 5 6 7 8 9 10

Printed in the United States of America

Thoroughly Covered and Completely Filled

DRENCHED

JEFF STANFORD

ARROWS & STONES

To my wife, Joy, my favorite person on the planet.

To Raven, Matt, Robin, and Pat, my daughters and their husbands (the sons Joy and I prayed into our lives). They are the most amazing in the world.

To Izabella, Violet, Charlotte, Blue, and Judah, my priceless grandchildren with whom I want to share my relationship with the Holy Spirit and with their rising generation. May you experience the greatest burning fire of Holy Spirit revival in the history of the universe.

CONTENTS

ACKNOWLEDGMENTS

My sincere thanks and appreciation to all those who generously shared their time, wisdom, and encouragement with me during the process of developing this book. Their names are too numerous for me to mention here.

A special thank you to my wife and daughters for their efforts in helping to put this work together—and to Four Rivers Media for all their coaching and publishing services.

FOREWORD

BY TONY D. STEWART

When I think of the word "drenched," I imagine everyone has experienced the feeling of being caught in an unexpected rainstorm and having to run across the parking lot to their cars. In a moment, our clothes are sopping wet.

There truly is a thirst in the Earth! Just as the dry ground cries for rain and the hungry crave food, there is a longing for the presence of God. There is an awakening today, just as Joel prophesied:

"I will pour out my Spirit on all people. Your sons and daughters will prophesy, your old men will dream dreams, and your young men will see visions. Even on my servants, both men and women, I will pour out my Spirit in those days" (Joel 2:28-29, NIV).

Fathers and mothers are being stirred. Sons and daughters are being equipped and sent. A mighty army is rising as an outpouring of the Holy Spirit is covering the Earth.

In *Drenched*, Jeff Stanford outlines in such a profound way the benefits of living a Spirit-filled life. After a detailed scriptural outline, he addresses these benefits, such as communication with the Spirit, how Spirit-led living enhances your daily walk as demonstrated through the fruits of the Spirit, supernatural gifts, guidance, a heavenly language, worship, intercession, companionship, ability to overcome, and comfort.

Pastor Jeff builds our faith and challenges us with kingdom principles to pursue God's presence, declaring, just like the prophet Elijah, that there is a sound of an abundance of rain and the heavens have been activated and are ready. My prayer for you, as you read this book, is for a fire to be ignited and a holy passion to be stirred as we are all "drenched" with the supernatural presence of God.

—Tony D. Stewart
Assistant General Overseer
Church of God International
Pastor, City Life Church
Tampa, Florida

FOREWORD

BY TOBY S. MORGAN

L ife presents us with a constant need for refreshing rain from the heavens. In fact, should the rains cease, as droughts reveal, life will soon disappear. However, amazing things transpire when the life-giving waters from the heavens fall upon parched Earth.

Once, when living in the beautiful city of Albuquerque, New Mexico, I witnessed first-hand what can occur when the heavens open and the arid landscape is drenched with water. An unusual early summer rainy period occurred. After the clouds disappeared and the sun's bright rays carpeted the Earth, long-hidden seeds erupted into a blanket of color, and the desert bloomed like a rose. Colors rarely seen in the desert suddenly burst upon the scene and added a luster to the beauty of the barren landscape.

That same scenario occurs when an individual allows the Holy Spirit unlimited access to their life. In *Drenched*, Pastor Jeff Stanford aptly describes the drenching power of the Holy Spirit. Following the illustration of Peter, who spoke of the Holy Ghost falling like rain from heaven on Gentile believers (Acts 11:15), and Jesus, who described the effect of the Holy Spirit in our lives in terms of multiple rivers (John 7:38), Pastor Stanford reveals how our lives can be drenched by the Spirit of God and erupt into a colorful landscape in the kingdom.

Revealing how the direction of his life was rerouted by the impact of this drenching presence from heaven, Pastor Stanford lends his voice to millions of believers around the globe who have witnessed amazing life change when finding themselves drenched by continual access to the fountains of spiritual water available to the believer (Isaiah 12:3). He presents a clear call for a renewal of thirst for a personal and intimate walk with the Holy Spirit that produces a life soaked by the intoxicating influence of the Spirit of God as well as a bountiful garden of evidence of His presence.

Read *Drenched* and allow the Rainmaker from Heaven to drench you in His presence. Do not run away from the clouds. Do not decide to stop His flow through your life to reset those things His floodtide presence disrupts. Stay put in His presence, and allow Him full access to your life as He guides you into a life marked by His drenching presence. Your life may occasionally get a little sloppy because of the rain, but the surprises awaiting you when He does His work in your life will be worth any cost.

—Toby S. Morgan
Administrative Bishop
Virginia Church of God

INTRODUCTION

Suddenly, He was there—in the room with me!

"In the last days," God says,
"I will pour out my Spirit upon all people.
Your sons and daughters will prophesy.
Your young men will see visions,
and your old men will dream dreams.
In those days I will pour out my Spirit
even on my servants—men and women alike—
and they will prophesy. —Acts 2:17-18 (NLT)

As a child growing up in the Pentecostal church, I heard a lot of teaching and preaching about what was right and what was wrong. I heard a lot about sin, worldliness, the devil, and a place called hell where a person would burn with fire forever and ever, and the fire would never go out. I was living with the impression that if I made a mistake or broke any of the church rules, I was backslidden, and if I died in that condition, I was going to hell. I sang the church songs, I said the prayers I had been taught to pray and prayers I had heard others pray, and I went to the altars over and over, asking God to forgive me and save me.

Finally, when I was sixteen years old, I went to the altar on a Sunday morning and encountered God. A true change took place in my heart, and I received a greater desire to please the Lord than I had ever experienced. Something supernatural occurred in my life, and I felt the change. It was like I had been given a new life, and I believe that was the moment I was genuinely born again (see John 3:1-21). From that moment, there was something on the inside of me that was hungry for more of God in my life. Something inside me wanted to live for God, serve God, worship God, know more about God, talk to God, feel God, and experience God all the time.

The church not only talked about salvation and being born again, but the church also talked a lot about being baptized in the Holy Spirit and speaking in other tongues (see Matthew 3:11 and Acts 2:1-4). I wanted everything God had to offer, so I began to pray daily for God to baptize me in His Holy Spirit. About three months later, during a revival service in the hot month of July in 1980, I received the baptism in the Holy Spirit and spoke in a spiritual language. It was an indescribable experience that lasted into the early hours of the morning.

I began praying for this experience every day, especially when I went to church. Like me, I saw many in the church who had received the baptism in the Holy Spirit, spoken in a spiritual language, and wanted more experiences with the Holy Spirit. I saw many in the church living the Christian life, going from spiritual experience to spiritual experience. The experiences were powerful and joyful, but in between the experiences, there was a lot of discouragement and defeat.

This began a journey of discovery and adventure for me with the Holy Spirit. There was something on the inside of me that kept saying, *There is more of God than what you have.* Every day, as I prayed, I would say to God, *I know there is more of you, and I want more!* I would pray to God, *Help me to know you better, to communicate with you better, and to be sensitive to Your presence in my life.* I knew that God was omnipresent, meaning He is everywhere at all times (see Psalm 139:7-10). I also knew that He was living in my heart, on the inside of me. But I desired more. I desired for God the Holy Spirit to manifest His presence in my life in a real, felt, and tangible way.

THE EXPERIENCES WERE POWERFUL AND JOYFUL, BUT IN BETWEEN THE EXPERIENCES, THERE WAS A LOT OF DISCOURAGEMENT AND DEFEAT.

One day, while I was home alone reading my Bible, I began to talk to the Holy Spirit. Now, this was unusual for me; I usually talked to God the Father and God the Son, but I had never addressed God the Holy Spirit. Suddenly, He was there, in the room with me! The Holy Spirit was as real to me as any person who ever sat beside me. I said to Him, *I know this is You, Holy Spirit, for I have been in your manifest presence before.*

I began to welcome Him and thank Him for making His presence real to me. It was an incredible experience that changed the focus and direction of my life. I'm not sure how long that experience lasted. I was overwhelmed by His presence. Scriptures began to come to me, and I began to ask Him about them. He gave me answers, opened my understanding, and taught me very simple and easy-to-understand things. It was like the whole world had been closed off, and I was in a special place, all alone with God, with His undivided attention.

I can't adequately describe this experience; it was love, joy, peace, and all the other wonderful things about inner fulfillment and satisfaction that you can imagine simultaneously. From that moment, the Holy Spirit became more alive in my life than I ever knew He could be. He was no longer just an encounter or an experience but more real than any human person I had ever known. I knew He was a real person, and He wanted to be my friend.

When you receive the Holy Spirit, you receive the greatest friend you will ever have! I have discovered that God the Holy Spirit wants to have more than encounters and experiences with us. He wants us to grow and mature through our encounters and experiences until we move into a day-in, day-out, hand-holding, neck-hugging relationship with Him.

I have discovered that all I need to do is acknowledge that He is everywhere and on the inside of me, and I'm not waiting for Him to show up or manifest in some tangible way. But He is waiting for me. He is with me and in me at all times, and He is a gentleman who will not intrude on me or force me in any way to do anything I'm not comfortable with; he is just waiting on me to acknowledge Him, invite Him, welcome Him, and yield my will to Him. He is ready to manifest Himself in my life. He is our Helper, our Comforter, and our Friend. He is giving us direction and leading us into truth and victory as we are willing to yield our will to Him (see John 16:13).

CHAPTER 1

THE DRENCHED LIFE

SOAKED IN HIS PRESENCE

My story of coming to Christ is unique in many ways. I mentioned already how a few days after my sixteenth birthday, I went to the altar on a Sunday morning and asked Jesus to forgive me of my sins. I gave Him the rest of my life, and something changed inside me that day. I began to sense the presence of Jesus living inside of me. It was the beginning of a genuine relationship with the God I had been taught about and knew a lot about, but now it was a living reality that God Himself was living inside me day in and day out. He was loving, encouraging, leading, and teaching me. I was walking with Him, and He was walking with me. I was talking with Him, and He was talking with me.

At that time, the church we were attending had a youth ministry that I enjoyed and attended regularly. I was encouraged and inspired by the leaders who were working with the teenagers. I was especially inspired by the prayer life and relationship with God I saw in them. I would watch and listen to them pray and talk to God as if He were a tangible person, and as they would pray, I could sense the presence of Jesus with us. I watched and learned from them how to talk and relate to God. I prayed daily and asked God to help me pray and have a relationship with Him like they had. And my relationship with God began to take off. I had a real drive to know God more and in a more personal way.

THE MORE I LEARNED, THE MORE I WANTED TO KNOW ABOUT HIM.

Every day, I would try to find private places to be alone with God, pray, sense, and learn His presence. In these times of prayer, I would always ask God for more of Him, and His presence would become real, as if I could feel Him touching me. I could tell when God wanted me to pray, and I would stop what I was doing and find a private place to be alone with Him. I was learning how to recognize and be sensitive to the God living in me. I was learning to acknowledge and respond to how things felt inside me when He wanted me to respond to Him. I was recognizing thoughts, feelings, and impressions that were from Him. Things inside me were becoming sensitive to His prompting. As I responded, I was learning to hear His voice. Each time I responded to His promptings to pray and spend time with Him, He would advise me about things in my life, and sometimes, He would give me instructions and directions about things He wanted me to do for

Him. I was learning more and more about Him. And the more I learned, the more I wanted to know more about Him.

These times of private prayer created a hunger and thirst for more of God in my life. I began to develop an inner desire to read the Bible. As I prayed and read, the Bible became as if it were a real person to me. A person that was almost tangible to me. The more I read the Bible, the hungrier I became. I began to make more time in my life for prayer and to read the Bible. I would also watch other Christians around me and see how God worked in their lives and used them in incredible ways.

In the summer of that year, after school was out, I had more time to give to prayer and to reading the Bible. I began to be aware of the God living in me as the Holy Spirit living in me. I began to talk with Him. I constantly asked the Holy Spirit for more of God in Jesus's name. I wanted the Holy Spirit to fill me until His presence ran over in my life. I was seeking more of God in private, but then I began to publicly seek more of God every time the pastor would open the altars for prayer. I began attending prayer services at the church, people's homes, or anywhere people gathered to pray.

One night, I went to the altar and began to pray again and ask Jesus to baptize me. A group of ladies who knew how to pray surrounded me, placed their hands on my head and shoulders, and began asking God to baptize me in the Holy Spirit. Late into the evening, I began to sense the presence of God move over me. It was like liquid electricity as it began to flow over me from my head down to my feet. I recognized this as the baptism in the Holy Spirit, and as I began to thank God for what was happening to me, my native language changed, and I knew it was the Holy

Spirit giving me a spiritual language. I cannot tell you how long I prayed in this new language, but this was only the beginning of the hand-holding, neck-hugging relationship I was discovering God wanted with me.

I am sharing these things with you because Jesus wants a real and powerful relationship with you. He wants to be the very best friend you will ever have. He wants to be able to advise you and give you special instructions and direction. He wants to lead you through the good times and the times that are not so good. But it all starts with asking Jesus to forgive you of all your sins, give you the ability to forsake all your sinful ways, come into your heart, fill you with His desires, and have His way.

This will be the most incredible and exciting journey of your life! That is what *Drenched* is all about: being "drenched" in God's presence and power. It is to help you begin your spiritual growth journey. The things you will learn in this book—if you put them into practice on a daily basis—will help you grow closer to God and become a person of strong faith and character.

THE THINGS YOU WILL LEARN IN THIS BOOK—IF YOU PUT THEM INTO PRACTICE ON A DAILY BASIS—WILL HELP YOU GROW CLOSER TO GOD AND BECOME A PERSON OF STRONG FAITH AND CHARACTER.

The Bible talks to us about baptism. As a matter of fact, the Bible teaches at least three times that God wants us to be baptized.

THE BAPTISM OF SALVATION

The Holy Spirit is the baptizer of salvation. First Corinthians 12:13 (NKJV) says, "For by one Spirit we were all baptized into one body—whether Jews or Greeks, whether slaves or free." Therefore, the Bible teaches that the Holy Spirit baptizes us into Christ Jesus. This can be called the baptism of the Holy Spirit. The Bible is clear: no man can come to the heavenly Father except through Christ Jesus, and no one can come to Christ except the Holy Spirit draws or brings them.

The Holy Spirit convicts our hearts of sin, draws us to Christ, and baptizes us into our salvation in Christ. This is the primary step in the baptism of salvation (see Acts 2:38). God wants us to be drenched in repentance. Repentance is more than just feeling bad about our mistakes, faults, shortcomings, and sins. Repentance is more than apologizing to God and others for the sinful way we have lived or the sins we have committed. Repentance is forsaking our sins and sinful ways, changing direction, and refusing to return to our previous or old way of living. Repentance is a changing of our minds and a determined will to allow Christ to live through us and represent Him and His righteousness.

God wants your salvation to be a complete drenching. He forgives you of all your sins. It is a complete baptism—total immersion. God wants you to be completely drenched in salvation. This is NOT the baptism IN the Holy Spirit.

THE BAPTISM IN WATER

The Bible teaches that after we have been baptized into Christ for salvation, we should follow Christ in water baptism. Water baptism is an outward expression of an inward change. It's a public declaration of how Jesus changed your life. Being baptized shows others that you've decided to follow Jesus and allows them to celebrate this decision with you (see 1 Corinthians 15:3-4 and Colossians 2:12).

WATER BAPTISM IS AN OUTWARD EXPRESSION OF AN INWARD CHANGE.

Baptism doesn't make you a believer; it shows that you already believe. Baptism doesn't save you; only your faith in Christ does that. Instead, baptism is a physical demonstration that testifies to the church and the world that we are willfully laying down our old sinful lives and taking up the new life that Jesus died on the cross to give us.

This is also a spiritual demonstration that testifies to us that Jesus is alive in us, and He wants to live His life through us. When we go under the water, we are testifying that our old person is dead and buried along with all its sins. When we come up out of the water, we are testifying that we are new persons in Christ Jesus, and we have new desires to love and serve Jesus. We have been given a new life in Christ Jesus. God wants us to be drenched when we're baptized in water.

THE BAPTISM IN THE HOLY SPIRIT

God wants us to be baptized into Christ. God wants us to be baptized in water. And God wants us to be baptized IN the Holy Spirit.

In Matthew 3:11 (KJV), John the Baptist referred to Jesus:

"I indeed baptize you with water unto repentance, but He who is coming after me is mightier than I, whose sandals I am not worthy to carry. He will baptize you with the Holy Spirit and fire."

At salvation, the Holy Spirit immerses you in Christ. At Spirit baptism, Jesus immerses you in the presence of the Holy Spirit. Jesus is the baptizer in the Holy Spirit.

John's statement here is one of just a handful of statements or accounts mentioned in all four Gospels—you can find the other three versions of this verse in Mark 1:8, Luke 3:16, and John 1:33. You'll find accounts of the death and resurrection of Jesus in all four Gospels, as these events are central to the gospel story and explain vital truths believers need to understand.

I believe it's significant that the baptism in the Holy Spirit is also in all four Gospels. Scripture clearly shows us Jesus is the one who performs this baptism, immersing us in the Holy Spirit (see Matthew 3:11, Acts 19:1-6, and 1 Corinthians 12:13). Yet because this baptism has been harmfully misrepresented, countless Christians avoid it. How could Jesus baptizing us in the Holy Spirit possibly be a bad thing, especially when it's so plainly present in the Bible?

This promise of the baptism in the Holy Spirit came powerfully to the disciples in Acts 2. Peter delivered a sermon immediately after the outpouring of the Holy Spirit on the day of Pentecost. In response to Peter's preaching, three thousand of his Jewish listeners fell under the conviction of the Holy Spirit:

Now when they heard this, they were cut to the heart, and said to Peter and the rest of the apostles, "Men and brethren, what shall we do?"

["What shall we do?" That's a pretty broad question. How does Peter respond?]

Then Peter said to them, "Repent, and let every one of you be baptized in the name of Jesus Christ for the remission of sins; and you shall receive the gift of the Holy Spirit. For the promise is to you and to your children, and to all who are afar off, as many as the Lord our God will call." —Acts 2:37-39 (NKJV)

Notice that in these verses, Peter outlined three baptisms. He said:

1) Repent.
2) Be baptized. (Peter urged his listeners to follow Jesus's example by submitting themselves to water baptism. See Acts 2:38-39.)
3) Receive the gift of the Holy Spirit.

This is the third baptism.

As Peter indicated, the Holy Spirit will not force Himself upon anyone. He must be "received."

From here on out, through the Word of God, the third baptism continually follows the first two as an essential, critical part of the Christian life. Today, God wants to empower you to overcome sin, the world, and the devil. God wants you to be baptized three times: into salvation, into water, and into His Holy Spirit.

When you are drenched or baptized IN the Holy Spirit, you will receive the Spirit like a wind and like fire. Acts 2:17-18 (KJV) is a prophecy as well as a promise for us today:

And it shall come to pass in the last days, saith God, I will
pour out of my Spirit upon all flesh: and your sons and your
daughters shall prophesy, and your young men shall see
visions, and your old men shall dream dreams:
And on my servants and on my handmaidens I will
pour out in those days of my Spirit; and they shall prophesy.

This prophecy and promise give us some insight into the person of God the Holy Spirit. In Acts 2, over one hundred people had gathered in an upper room in Jerusalem when the Holy Spirit came with the sound of a mighty rushing wind and filled the whole house where they were sitting. The Bible doesn't say that the Holy Spirit is the wind but that He can manifest Himself like the wind. Wind cannot be seen, but its effects can be felt and heard—just like the Holy Spirit. We cannot see Him, but we can feel the effects of His presence and His power.

On the day of Pentecost, Acts 2:2 (NIV) says, "And suddenly there came a sound from heaven as of a rushing mighty wind, and it filled all the house where they were sitting." Wind is a great word to describe the power of the Holy Spirit. Change happens when winds blow, and when the Holy Spirit moves, He brings change like wind. Wind produces energy, and when the Holy Spirit moves like the wind, He produces super-natural energy in us. He empowers us to do what we cannot naturally do alone. Oh, how we need the supernatural wind of the Holy Spirit!

Then, what looked like tongues of fire sat upon the heads of each of them. The Bible doesn't say that the Holy Spirit is tongues of fire but that the Holy Spirit can manifest Himself as tongues of fire. Every person in the upper room was filled with the Holy Spirit and spoke in various languages as the Holy Spirit gave them the ability. This proves that God the Holy Spirit can break through every communication barrier and make Himself real to anyone.

Many things happened to those receiving this great outpouring of the Holy Spirit. They were filled with incredible unity. They were filled with great joy. So much joy that when they came out of the upper room down onto the streets of Jerusalem, the people thought they were drunken.

They were baptized in the Holy Spirit.

They were filled and overflowing with the Holy Spirit.

They were completely immersed in the Holy Spirit, like being plunged into a river of free-flowing water.

They were totally drenched in the Holy Spirit.

Drenched means they were thoroughly covered and completely filled to overflowing. This is what God wants for us. He wants us to be thoroughly covered and completely filled to overflowing with His presence. Then, they were filled with great boldness. And Peter, full of the Spirit and boldness, began to preach, and three thousand people gave their lives to Jesus Christ.

As Peter preached, he said that this was what the prophet Joel prophesied—that in the last days, God would pour His Spirit out on all people, young and old, male and female, and that all would prophesy. Peter said that the church received an outpouring of the Holy Spirit, which was the former rain. Yes, the Bible describes the Holy Spirit as rain, falling on us from heaven. Falling on us, pouring down on us, drenching us with the Holy Spirit.

DRENCHED MEANS THEY WERE THOROUGHLY COVERED AND COMPLETELY FILLED TO OVERFLOWING.

The Bible also teaches that in the last days, we will experience the former rain and the latter rain at the same time (see Joel 2:23). The former rain came at seed time, and the latter rain came at harvest time. The former rain came right after the seed had been put into the ground; then there was a waiting season, and then a latter rain came that caused the seed to sprout and spring up and produce fruit. However, the Bible says that in the last days, the former and the latter rain will come at the same time, meaning that in the last days, God will accelerate the process and reduce the wait time.

If you are willing to allow the rain to fall on you, God is willing to speed up the process and produce the fruit of His presence and glory in you. I'm talking about allowing God to baptize you with His Holy Spirit until you are completely drenched and overflowing, running over with His presence and glory.

You will receive a supernatural unity with fellow believers. After the day of Pentecost, there was incredible unity among those approximately 120 believers gathered in one place and with one accord—all moving in the same direction, all focused on the same purpose. Men and women prayed together, sought God together, united and moved in the same direction, and focused on the same purpose.

You will receive incredible joy like unto drunkenness or intoxication.

You will receive boldness to withstand the temptation, adversity, and opposition that Satan brings against you. You will also receive the boldness to be life-changing witnesses for Christ Jesus.

I want you to ask yourself an important question: Have you experienced only two baptisms? Have you ever experienced an immersion in the Holy Spirit that brought supernatural power and help into your life?

Jesus wants to baptize you with power from on high (see Luke 24:49). Why in the world would anyone say "Thanks, but no thanks!" to that? Listen to what He says in Luke 11:9-13 (NKJV):

> *"So I say to you, ask, and it will be given to you; seek, and you will find; knock, and it will be opened to you. For everyone who asks receives, and he who seeks finds, and to him who knocks it will be opened. If a son asks for bread from any father among you, will he give him a stone? Or if he asks for a fish, will he give him a serpent instead of a fish? Or if he asks for an egg, will he offer him a scorpion? If you then, being evil, know how to give good gifts to your*

*children, how much more will your heavenly Father give
the Holy Spirit to those who ask Him!"*

Jesus tells us if our earthly fathers can give us good gifts, "How much more will your heavenly Father give the Holy Spirit to those who ask Him!"

THE BIBLE IS CLEAR THAT THE HOLY SPIRIT IS A PERSON. HE CAME TO EARTH, PEOPLE RECEIVED HIM, AND HE HAS NOT LEFT. HE IS STILL HERE AND LIVES IN EVERYONE WHO WILL BE BORN AGAIN AND RECEIVE HIM.

Many people have misconceptions about being baptized in the Holy Spirit. Some have been told that this baptism died with the apostles and was only for their day. But the Bible is clear that the Holy Spirit is a person. He came to Earth, people received Him, and He has not left. He is still here and lives in everyone who will be born again and receive Him. Jesus wants us to be thoroughly covered and completely filled to overflowing with the presence of the Holy Spirit—*drenched!*

Jesus also says that everyone who asks will receive, everyone who seeks will find, and to everyone who will knock, the door will open to them. He means we should ask and keep on asking, seek and keep on seeking, knock and keep on knocking until we receive, until we find, and until the door to this supernatural relationship opens to us.

Some people have been told that this baptism of the Holy Spirit is of the devil. But Jesus says we do not have to be afraid to ask. If you ask, you will not receive the wrong thing. If you, being evil, know how to give good gifts to your children, how much more will your heavenly Father give the Holy Spirit to those asking Him!

Jesus asks if your children ask you for bread, will you give them a stone? Of course not! If your children ask you for fish, will you give them a serpent? Of course not! If your children ask you for an egg, will you give them a scorpion? Of course not! Neither do we have to be afraid we will receive the wrong thing! We do not have to be afraid we will receive something other than the genuine, authentic person of the Holy Spirit Himself. Jesus says you will receive what you ask for. If you ask for bread, you will receive bread. If you ask for fish, you will receive fish, if you ask for an egg, you will receive an egg, and if you ask for the Holy Spirit, you will receive exactly what you ask for—you will receive the Holy Spirit!

So, don't be afraid; don't be held back by misconceptions any longer! Don't allow anyone to mislead you in any way! Jesus is the great baptizer in the Holy Spirit, and He wants you to be thoroughly covered, completely filled, and overflowing with the Holy Spirit!

In John 7:37-39 (NKJV), Jesus, the great baptizer, makes us this promise:

> *"If anyone thirsts, let him come to Me and drink. He who believes in Me, as the Scripture has said, out of his heart*

will flow rivers of living water." But this He spoke con-
cerning the Spirit, whom those believing in Him would
receive; for the Holy Spirit was not yet given because Jesus
was not yet glorified.

Don't listen to anyone else on this matter; listen only to Jesus!
Jesus is the great baptizer! Every born-again believer should
be hungry and thirsty to receive everything Jesus has for us!
Many Christians are living lives of defeat, frustration, and
failure: "But you shall receive power when the Holy Spirit has
come upon you" (Acts 1:8, KJV). That's a biblical truth that can
transform you.

Many believers live from spiritual high to spiritual high, experiencing lots of discouragement and disappointment in between.
But when you are drenched, thoroughly covered and completely
filled with the Holy Spirit and develop this friendship and fellowship with Him daily, He gives you the courage and confidence
you need in the low times.

MANY BELIEVERS LIVE FROM SPIRITUAL HIGH TO SPIRITUAL HIGH, EXPERIENCING LOTS OF DISCOURAGEMENT AND DISAPPOINTMENT IN BETWEEN.

Will you pray and receive the Holy Spirit today?

*Dear Lord Jesus, I believe with all my heart that You want
to baptize me in the Holy Spirit. I'm asking You to baptize
me in the Holy Spirit. By faith, I receive this baptism, give
the Holy Spirit control of my life, and allow Him to have
His way in me. I will be sensitive to Him living in me and
allow Him to burn in my heart, flow through my mind,
see through my eyes, hear through my ears, speak through
my mouth, and use my hands and feet as His very own.
My body is His temple, and I invite, welcome, and receive
the Holy Spirit in all His fullness. In Jesus's name!*

Now, lift your heart and voice to God and begin thanking Him for His presence. Worship Him with your whole heart, and give Him praise for what He is doing. Get alone with God, pray to and worship Him simply because He is God—for no other reason. Watch the intimacy grow and the power of your emotions lessen.

THE MORE SENSITIVE YOU ARE TO HIM AND FOLLOW HIS COMMANDS AND COUNSEL, THE STRONGER, MORE STABLE, POWERFUL, AND VICTORIOUS YOU WILL BECOME.

As you develop this kind of relationship with God the Holy Spirit, begin to recognize that you are thoroughly covered and completely filled—drenched—with the presence of the Holy

Spirit. The Holy Spirit will provide and develop within you a strong security that God is present, with you and in you. He is active and on duty 24/7—despite the ups and downs that will come your way.

Once you receive the baptism in the Holy Spirit, your intimacy with the person of the Spirit grows, and you continue to develop this personal relationship with God. There will be a continuing transformation process that will move you away from reliance on feelings and emotions. Instead, you will develop strong stability, knowing that your emotions do not dictate His involvement in your life. He is always with you! He is with you when you feel good and when you are not feeling so good. He is with you when you are happy, sad, or even mad. He is with you when you are weak and when you are strong. He is always there waiting for you to acknowledge Him and rely on Him for His guidance, direction, and comfort in all life's ups and downs and emotional traumas and dramas. The more sensitive you are to Him and follow His commands and counsel, the stronger, more stable, powerful, and victorious you will become.

If this book is in your hands and you have never asked Jesus to save you, I would like to invite you to pray like I prayed to become a follower of Christ.

Dear Lord Jesus, I know I am a sinner and ask for Your forgiveness. I believe You died for my sins and rose from the dead as it says in Romans 10:9. I will trust and follow You as my Lord and Savior. Guide my life and help me to do Your will. In Your name. Amen.

CHAPTER 2

COMMUNION WITH THE HOLY SPIRIT

FRIENDSHIP THAT BRINGS VICTORY

Many are trying to live a victorious Christian life without an intimate relationship with the Holy Spirit. Many Christians have been baptized and filled and refilled and refilled but still are not enjoying the victory. This is because we've had experiences with the Holy Spirit, but God intends that we go on to discover and explore the greatest adventure this side of heaven (a hand-holding, neck-hugging relationship with the Holy Spirit).

WE NEED COMMUNION WITH THE HOLY SPIRIT

The apostle Paul was one of the greatest Spirit-filled men of God we will ever read about in the Bible. He had a lot to say to us about God the Holy Spirit. Paul was a missionary, evangelist, and church planter. One of the churches he started was the church in the city of Corinth. If you read through the two letters of Corinthians, you will discover that the church at Corinth had many problems, and Paul continuously had to deal with issues in the church.

In 2 Corinthians 13:11-14, as the apostle Paul is giving his final farewell, as he signs his benediction, he gives them the key to victory in every battle and the solution to every problem they will ever face in the future:

> *Finally, brethren, farewell. Become complete. Be of good comfort, be of one mind, live in peace; and the God of love and peace will be with you. Greet one another with a holy kiss. All the saints greet you. The grace of the Lord Jesus Christ, and the love of God, and the communion of the Holy Spirit be with you all. Amen.*
> *—2 Corinthians 13:11-14 (NKJV)*

Here are Paul's encouragement and instructions: *Stay in the grace of the Lord Jesus Christ.* We are saved by grace, and to have victory in this life, you must also *stay* in the grace of the Lord Jesus Christ.

No matter what you are going through, stay in grace.

No matter how difficult life can be, stay in grace.

Grace is God's undeserved favor. If you have received God's grace, God wants you to extend His grace to others. Being in grace means being gracious to others who do not deserve your favor or kindness. This is a significant key to victory in this life. Being gracious to others keeps you in fellowship with the Holy Spirit.

We must be gracious at all times, in all circumstances, and with all people.

- Be gracious when you are irritated.
- Be gracious when you are frustrated.
- Be gracious when you are anxious, nervous, or fearful.
- Be gracious when you are sad, disappointed, and discouraged.
- Be gracious when you are glad, happy, successful, and blessed.

Being gracious to others keeps you in fellowship with the Holy Spirit.

GRACE IS GOD'S UNDESERVED FAVOR. IF YOU HAVE RECEIVED GOD'S GRACE, GOD WANTS YOU TO EXTEND HIS GRACE TO OTHERS.

STAY IN LOVE WITH GOD THE FATHER

Love the Lord your God with all of your heart, your soul, your mind, and all your strength. And love others with the same love that Christ has been loving you. You do not love God if you do not love others. You love God by loving others, especially those who do not deserve your love and those who will not return your love. Even love your enemies—not just the folks who love you back. While you are being gracious to others, the love of God is manifesting in you toward God and others.

As you are gracious to others, loving others, especially the unlovable, it keeps you in fellowship with the Holy Spirit.

- Love your enemies.
- Love those who talk about you.
- Love those who disagree with you.
- Love those that you disagree with.
- Love those who persecute you.
- Love those who criticize you.

- Love those who complain about you.
- Love those who gossip about you.
- Love those who hurt you.
- Love those who offend you.
- Love those who misuse you.

This does not mean that you put yourself in a position to be mistreated or abused. To love them means that you sincerely pray for them, ask God to bless them, and sincerely mean it with all your heart. As you are gracious to others, loving others, especially the unlovable, it keeps you in fellowship with the Holy Spirit.

AS YOU ARE GRACIOUS TO OTHERS, LOVING OTHERS, ESPECIALLY THE UNLOVABLE, IT KEEPS YOU IN FELLOWSHIP WITH THE HOLY SPIRIT.

STAY IN THE COMMUNION OF THE HOLY SPIRIT

God desires that you be in a hand-holding, neck-hugging, day-in, day-out relationship with the Holy Spirit. God the Holy Spirit wants to walk with you and talk with you every day, all throughout the day, and every night.

God the Holy Spirit wants you to recognize Him and acknowledge Him with you all the time; He is never leaving you. He is always with you.

God the Holy Spirit wants to lead you into all the blessings of the Lord.

God the Holy Spirit wants to give you His wisdom and knowledge to make you successful and victorious daily.

God the Holy Spirit is a real person that wants to be real to you.

He wants you to yield your will to Him and allow His will to be done in you.

He wants you to invite and welcome Him into your life; He will not intrude or force Himself on you.

He wants to be treated like He is with you.

He wants you to look to Him for His advice.

He wants you to talk with Him and enjoy His presence all the time.

He wants you to completely yield to Him and allow Him to have His way in your life.

He wants to fill your mind with His thoughts and your mouth with His words.

He wants to see through your eyes and hear through your ears.

He wants to live in your heart.

He wants to work through your hands and feet.

He wants you to give yourself to Him.

Pray this prayer every morning:

Good morning, Holy Spirit. Thank You so much for being with me. I know You have incredible plans for today, and I want to help You with those plans. As I go through this day, I want to follow You as you lead me. I give myself to You now; take me in Your hands as an instrument that You can use to accomplish Your plans through me. Amen.

Many Christ believers and followers are trying to live a victorious Christian life without an intimate relationship with the Holy Spirit! We've had experiences with the Holy Spirit, but God's intention is that we go on to discover and explore the greatest adventure this side of Heaven (a hand-holding, neck-hugging relationship with the Holy Spirit). We need communion with the Holy Spirit! This was Paul's instruction-filled farewell to the Corinthian church.

DEVELOP A HEALTHIER AND MORE POWERFUL RELATIONSHIP WITH OUR HEAVENLY FATHER THROUGH THE PERSON OF THE HOLY SPIRIT.

The English word communion translates from the Greek word *koinonia* and has a seven-fold meaning. As we look at them, we discover how to develop a healthier and more powerful relationship with our heavenly Father through the person of the Holy Spirit.

First of all, the word communion means *presence*. This is the first level. God the Father's desire for you is that the sweet presence of the Holy Spirit be with you. To enjoy the presence of the Holy Spirit, we must acknowledge that He is with us continually (if you are a born-again believer and have asked Jesus to baptize you in the Holy Spirit and have a willing and obedient spirit). As Christ believers and followers, we must recognize the Holy Spirit as a person constantly abiding with us and in us, never leaving us. We must consistently converse with the Holy Spirit, asking for His assistance, advice, instructions and directions throughout our everyday life and give Him priority to assist and direct us in everything life brings to us.

This incredible, invisible person (the Holy Spirit) is waiting for us to permit Him to lead us. He is ready to work through us the wonderful works of Christ. So, I challenge you to give yourself to the Holy Spirit continually and allow Him to work through you to fulfill the mission of Christ every day.

Learning this first step is incredibly exciting and life-changing! As you practice this step, be ready for unspeakable joy and boldness to invade you and be careful not to overdose others with this new fire, but harness this fire and allow the Holy Spirit to work gently with you to touch others around you.

The second meaning gives us our next step in our relationship with the Holy Spirit. Communion means *fellowship*. You must do more than just pray to, for, or through the Holy Spirit. You must fellowship with Him. You must spend time with Him. You must enjoy Him and allow Him to enjoy you. You should seek fellowship with Him. You must seek after this fellowship as you would for a drink of water while running the last leg of a marathon. It takes a deep hunger and thirst for the manifest presence of the Holy Spirit to experience fellowship with Him.

Go to your heavenly Father in prayer and thank Him for sending the Holy Spirit to be your helper. Acknowledge that the Holy Spirit is with you and living in you. Thank your Lord Jesus Christ for baptizing you in the Holy Spirit and with fire. Ask the Holy Spirit to assist you as you worship your heavenly Father in

Jesus's name. Maybe play some worship music and spend some time with your heavenly Father and your Savior, Jesus Christ, through the person of the Holy Spirit. Talk to Him and allow Him to talk with you. Enjoy your time together. Make this your daily lifestyle. And the Holy Spirit will walk alongside you continually. He will direct you, lead you, and encourage you. It's the way your heavenly Father intends for you to live.

Heavenly Father, I pray for my friends today. I ask You to encourage them, help them, and bless them with a deeper and more intimate relationship with You through the person of the Holy Spirit. Give them the peace to enjoy their relationship with God the Holy Spirit. In Jesus's name, I pray. Amen.

The third meaning of the word communion gives us the next step in our relationship with the Holy Spirit. This word communion means sharing together. In the early church, Christ's followers were sharing together with each other and with the Holy Spirit. Acts 15:28 (KJV) says, "For it seemed good to the Holy Ghost, and to us, to lay upon you no greater burden than these necessary things." In this passage of scripture, the apostles are writing to Christ's followers in the city of Antioch. They were sharing, even writing letters together.

To enjoy your relationship with God the Holy Spirit, you must acknowledge and recognize the presence of the Holy Spirit with you and then begin to share life with Him.

As you share your life with God the Holy Spirit, He will begin to share His life with you.

You pour out your heart to Him, and He will pour His heart out to you.

You share your desires with Him, and He will share His desires with you.

You share your sadness with Him, and He will share His gladness with you.

You share your needs with Him, and He will share His supply with you.

You share your brokenness with Him, and He will share His healing with you.

You share your troubles with Him, and He will share His deliverance with you.

You share your problems with Him, and He will share His solutions with you.

You share your discouragement with Him, and He will share His joy with you.

You share your fears with Him, and He will share His courage with you.

As you open yourself up to Him, He will open Himself up to you.

You share with Him, and He will share with you.

To get to the next level in your relationship with the Holy Spirit, don't hold anything back from Him. Say the following, *Hello, Holy Spirit*, and then begin sharing your life with Him. The negative drag of this earthly life will begin to lose its grip on you as you share your whole self with the Holy Spirit.

Now, let's talk about the fourth step in our relationship with the Holy Spirit. The fourth meaning of the word communion is *participation*. Every day, as we acknowledge the presence of the Holy Spirit continually with us and we share our lives with him, the Holy Spirit will partner with us as we yield ourselves to Him (or give in to His leading). The Holy Spirit is ready to lead us and guide us in our daily lives. But He will not intrude on us, override our will, or try to force us in any way to participate with Him. He will gently nudge us and give us inner promptings in an effort to instruct us, encourage us, and direct us.

> **THE NEGATIVE DRAG OF THIS EARTHLY LIFE WILL BEGIN TO LOSE ITS GRIP ON YOU AS YOU SHARE YOUR WHOLE SELF WITH THE HOLY SPIRIT.**

What He wants from us is our willful participation in those promptings. As we give in to those promptings or as we yield ourselves to His guidance and participate with Him, we begin to learn how to follow Him and develop a closer and stronger relationship with Him. Be aware that you still have your own personal desires, and many times, our personal desires struggle against the Holy Spirit's desires. The struggle is in overriding our own personal desires and giving in to the Holy Spirit's desires. We must develop the ability to know the difference between our own will and desires and the Holy Spirit's will and desires.

Many times, our will and way are much stronger than the prompting and leading of the Holy Spirit (we are all in a battle with selfishness). And in those times, we are prone to follow our own will, and we must be careful not to miss the Holy Spirit's direction. The Holy Spirit and you become partners in life. You allow Him to give you the instructions, and you participate with a willing and obedient attitude.

The Bible is littered with passages like, "The Spirit with us," and "The Holy Spirit working with us," making it clear that the Holy Spirit is participating with us. Let me pray with you.

Heavenly Father, I pray in the name of Jesus that You will help us to recognize the presence of the Holy Spirit continually with us and help us to share our lives with Him and learn how to participate with Him in our everyday lives. And may our relationship with You grow stronger and closer as we participate with the Holy Spirit.

The fifth meaning of the word communion in 2 Corinthians 13:14 means intimacy. As we look at this word communion, we are learning how to develop a closer and more intimate relationship with our heavenly Father, through the person of the Holy Spirit. We are taking steps together in an attempt to interact with the person of the Holy Spirit.

The first step is to acknowledge and recognize the presence of the Holy Spirit with us continually; then we take the next step by fellowshipping with Him, enjoying Him, and allowing Him to enjoy us, and then by opening ourselves up and pouring out our hearts to Him. Hold nothing back, but share your heart with Him and allow Him to share His heart with you. As we continue to learn and grow to walk with Him and talk with Him, we begin to participate with Him. When He moves, we move. When He speaks, we speak. When He stops, we stop, etc. As we are participating with the Holy Spirit, we will walk right into the next step.

The next step in our relationship with the Holy Spirit is *intimacy*. This is a spiritual and supernatural intimacy that can only be realized in a close and consistent relationship with the Holy Spirit. This is realized as a supernatural love that is beyond the kinds of love that can be experienced in this present world, but a love that is only given by God Himself to us, through the Holy Spirit. You'll never know a deep love with Christ until you know it with the Holy Spirit who brings that intimacy, like in Romans 5:5 (KJV): "The love of God is shed abroad in our hearts by the Holy Ghost which is given to us." There is no other way. You cannot have an intimate love with God without a personal, active, consistent relationship with the Holy Spirit.

We are intimate with the Holy Spirit through our prayers and meditation on the Word of God and by giving ourselves completely and unreserved in thanksgiving, praise, worship, and rejoicing inwardly as well as outwardly and without shame, but with great faith, great trust, and confidence in God. As we are faithfully intimate with the Holy Spirit, He imparts and reveals Himself to us in incredible and sometimes even indescribable ways. As we are intimate in our worship and prayer (the spiritual oxygen that produces spiritual life), the Holy Spirit conceives in us His great plans and desires His will for us. His call on our lives will be activated, and His anointing that enables us to fulfill His will empowers us. His strength and wisdom will be added to our efforts to accomplish great things for the kingdom of God.

Lift your hands, begin to give yourself to the Holy Spirit in worship and prayer right now, and let me pray for you.

Heavenly Father, in Jesus's name, as we pray and worship You, we ask You to fill us with Your Holy Spirit until we move into a closer and more intimate relationship with You. We know Your presence is with us right now and never leaves us, we pour our hearts out to You and we receive all that You desire for us. Whatever You desire to do, we want to participate and work together with You to accomplish Your plans. Impart into us and conceive in us Your purpose, will, and desire for our lives. Thank You, heavenly Father, for loving us, blessing us, and using us to fulfill Your plans on the earth. Amen!

The sixth meaning of communion is *friendship*. The Bible is clear that no one can come to the Father, except through Jesus Christ! And no one can come to Christ unless the Holy Spirit draws them toward Him. So, as we acknowledge the presence of the Holy Spirit continually with us and in us, the Holy Spirit draws us along and we take steps together. The Holy Spirit is leading the way. He is giving us instructions. We are taking the steps together because the Holy Spirit wants us to develop a close and intimate relationship with Him. One of the ultimate goals of the Holy Spirit is to become your friend and for you to become His friend—best friends.

The Holy Spirit longs to be your closest friend. A friend is someone you have developed a great trust and confidence in, someone that you are loyal to, and someone who is loyal to you, and someone with whom you can share the deepest secrets of your heart. He will never betray your trust in Him.

THE HOLY SPIRIT LONGS TO BE YOUR CLOSEST FRIEND.

We are all only as sick as our secrets. But, we all know that it is not safe to share our secrets with just anyone, or with everybody. Your secrets are not only safe with the Holy Spirit, but as you share your secrets with Him, He will help you deal with the things that may be keeping you from moving forward. As you share your secrets with your friend, God the Holy Spirit, He helps you overcome obstacles, recover from sins and mistakes, break habits, remove barriers, and tear down inner walls and patterns of thinking that may be affecting your ability to succeed.

The Holy Spirit wants to be your friend. Pray with me now and let your heavenly Father know that you desire to be better friends with Him, and you want Him to be your very best friend.

Heavenly Father, I thank You so much for wanting to be my friend. I want to be Your friend. I want us to be close enough to share my deepest secrets with You and receive Your advice, instructions, and healing for every area of my life. I ask You in Jesus's name! Amen!

As we continue to look at the word communion found in 2 Corinthians 13:14, I want us to focus on its seventh and final meaning: commander. This means that the person of God the Holy Spirit is the commander. He must be in charge. He is like a captain or ruler and supervisor. However, He is a friendly one. He will not force us to follow His commands. We must ask for His instruction, and then we must allow Him to give us the instructions or call the shots. He wants to be in command. But He will not force us to give Him control. He will only become the commander of our life when we surrender complete control to Him. Just like He commanded the apostles where to go and what to do, He must be allowed to rule in our personal affairs.

GOD THE HOLY SPIRIT IS THE HIGHEST INTELLIGENCE IN THE UNIVERSE, LIVING IN EVERY BORN-AGAIN BELIEVER, AND READY AND AVAILABLE TO HELP US IN EVERY WAY WE NEED HELP, BUT WE MUST SURRENDER CONTROL.

God the Holy Spirit is the highest intelligence in the universe, living in every born-again believer, and ready and available to help us in every way we need help, but we must surrender control. We must allow Him to call the shots if we want to see His perfect will accomplished in us and in the people He wants to reach through us.

Remember, when Jesus ascended to heaven and took His place at our heavenly Father's right hand, He asked the Father to send the Holy Spirit to us. The Holy Spirit appeared in the upper room in Jerusalem, filled those gathered there, and is still filling every believer who asks and surrenders their whole lives to Him. Our heavenly Father and our Savior and Lord, Jesus Christ, have put God the Holy Spirit in charge on the earth until Jesus returns! Our success in this life and in the life to come depends on the relationship we have with our heavenly Father and the Lord Jesus Christ through the person of the Holy Spirit.

Every day, include the Holy Spirit in everything you do. Every day, recognize His presence is always with you. Don't be afraid to talk to Him and ask Him for His advice and then follow His instructions. He is the very wisdom of God and will always lead you to succeed.

Pray this prayer with me:

Dear heavenly Father and Lord Jesus Christ, thank You so much for sending the Holy Spirit to be with me and lead me into the greatest adventure this side of heaven. Please help me to be more sensitive to the Holy Spirit and His presence in my life. In Jesus's name, I pray. Amen.

Now that we have looked at communion in 2 Corinthians 13:14 and its meanings, let's bring all these meanings together and look at how they help us develop and build a strong relationship with God the Holy Spirit. When we wake up each day, we should begin our day recognizing and acknowledging the presence of the Holy Spirit with us by speaking to Him and greeting Him at the very beginning of our day. It's okay to speak to Him. God the Holy Spirit is just as much God as God the Father and God the Son. If it's okay to speak to God the Father and God the Son, then it is okay to speak to God the Holy Spirit.

God the Holy Spirit was promised to us by God the Father, and God the Son requested the Father to send God the Holy Spirit to us. God the Holy Spirit is on the earth with us and He wants to have a relationship with us and that includes having conversations with us. We can speak to Him, and He will speak to us as well.

After we acknowledge Him, we should begin to fellowship with Him throughout the day through prayer, thanksgiving, praise, and worship. We should share everything with God the Holy Spirit throughout the day. As we do we will grow closer and closer to Him. We will begin to learn more about Him and how He desires to operate in our life. As we learn more and more about Him and how He desires to operate in our life we will begin to recognize His movements, we will learn more about His personality, and we will begin to understand how He loves us and how He wants us to love others. As we develop this trusting relationship and we give our will over to Him, He will begin to prompt and urge us to do things for Him. Then, as we participate with Him, we will see Him manifest Himself in us and in those He desires to reach and bless through us.

It is very important to read the Bible continually, over and over again and again. Reading the Bible on a daily basis is essential in your relationship with the Holy Spirit. The Holy Spirit will never step out of the boundaries of what He has already written in the Bible. Whatever the Holy Spirit says or does will always be in complete alignment with the Holy Scriptures. Continually reading the Bible will keep us from being misled by any other influence and help to keep our human spirit in line with the Holy Spirit. Day after day as we continue practicing this over and over and learn how to stay continuously engaged with God the Holy Spirit, we will develop a much closer relationship with Him until He becomes to us our closest and most trusted friend.

> **WHATEVER THE HOLY SPIRIT SAYS OR DOES WILL ALWAYS BE IN COMPLETE ALIGNMENT WITH THE HOLY SCRIPTURES. CONTINUALLY READING THE BIBLE WILL KEEP US FROM BEING MISLED BY ANY OTHER INFLUENCE.**

As we enjoy each other's friendship, He will begin to gently lead us and give us instruction. As we surrender control of ourselves to Him and allow Him to be in charge, He will give us commands. As we obey His commands, we will see Him supernaturally perform signs, wonders, and miracles in our lives and in the lives of those He desires to touch through us.

God the Holy Spirit never pushes or forces Himself on anyone, but He is patiently waiting on us to acknowledge Him, yield ourselves to Him, and give in to His desire for us. God the Holy

Spirit is very sensitive and easily pushed away. He can be grieved, resisted, quenched, and rejected, so be very careful, respectful, and reverent toward Him. He is God living in you.

Pray with me:

Dear heavenly Father, thank You so much for sending the Holy Spirit to me. Please teach me how to have the kind of relationship with Him that You desire for me to have. Help me to be sensitive to Him continually and in every way. May the Holy Spirit use me to bring glory to Your name. Amen.

CHAPTER 3

UNDER THE INFLUENCE

AN INTOXICATING RELATIONSHIP

T his drenching relationship you are developing with the Holy Spirit is continuing to fill you and overflow out of you, affecting everything about you. It is now becoming intoxicating. Like with a drunk person, this drenching is affecting every part of you: how you see, hear, speak, and walk out your life with the Holy Spirit as your constant, abiding friend. I believe God is—right now—pouring out His Holy Spirit on those who are hungry, thirsty, and available for more of Him in their lives. The apostle Paul said for us not to be drunk with the wine of this world, but be filled or drunk with the Holy Spirit: "And be not drunk with wine, wherein is excess; but be filled with the Spirit" (Ephesians 5:18).

The word intoxicate, according to *Webster's Dictionary,* means to make drunk, to be elated with enthusiasm or madness; delirious with excitement, to overdose, excessive, more than enough. God wants His relationship with us to be elated with enthusiasm and excitement. On the day of Pentecost, as they waited in that upper room in Jerusalem, they were all filled with incredible joy. They came out of that upper room "under the influence." We need to live under the influence of the Holy Spirit. (Instead of a DUI, we have an LUI—Living under the influence of the Spirit.)

I BELIEVE GOD IS—RIGHT NOW— POURING OUT HIS HOLY SPIRIT ON THOSE WHO ARE HUNGRY, THIRSTY, AND AVAILABLE FOR MORE OF HIM IN THEIR LIVES.

When you are intoxicated with the Holy Spirit, the Spirit life flows, just like Psalm 23 expresses with our cup overflowing. Romans 12:2 says that when you are intoxicated with the Holy Spirit, the Spirit overflows, through the avenues of your mind and through the process of renewing the mind. The Holy Spirit will renew the deep places of your heart with great power (or excessive force, deep throbbing). The person of the Holy Spirit is living inside of you, and you will sense His prompting, urging, nudges, like something on the inside of you telling you to go ahead. (A divine nudge?)

When you are under the influence of the Holy Spirit or intoxicated, you are so filled with a holy passion, fire, zeal, and excitement of the grace of God that you are illuminated or radiated by the power of this new wine until your whole being is intoxicated. You feel as if you have been raptured, you have been so caught up in the Spirit or carried away in the Spirit. The natural mind and the natural body cannot comprehend or contain all that's happening to a person who is under the influence of the Holy Spirit.

The Holy Spirit is the very presence of Jesus Christ on planet Earth in us—in our bodies—for our bodies are the temple of the Holy Spirit. The life, ministry, and relationship of Jesus Christ in this world are being carried, preserved, and activated in our mortal bodies until Christ returns; then, we too, shall be like Him. To be filled with the Spirit, intoxicated, or under the influence is to be the closest possible to Christ and to be the most possible like Christ. Our heavenly Father wants us to get drunk on this new wine! You do not get drunk by accident! If you get drunk, you get drunk on purpose! You must be intentional in your pursuit of this intoxicating relationship.

A true drunk does not like to drink alone (on the day of Pentecost over one hundred people got drunk together, remember?), and God wants us to drink this new wine with others. This is why it is so important to make yourself a part of a Spirit-filled church and be faithful to attend the gatherings, get involved, and serve in all the ways you can. Every opportunity to serve the body of Christ is also an opportunity for the Holy Spirit to operate in you.

EVERY OPPORTUNITY TO SERVE THE BODY OF CHRIST IS ALSO AN OPPORTUNITY FOR THE HOLY SPIRIT TO OPERATE IN YOU.

John 7:37-39 (NKJV) describes it like this:

> *On the last* day, *that great day of the feast, Jesus stood and cried out, saying, "If anyone thirsts, let him come to Me and drink. He who believes in Me, as the Scripture has said, out of his heart will flow rivers of living water." But this He spoke concerning the Spirit, whom those believing in Him would receive; for the Holy Spirit was not yet given because Jesus was not yet glorified.*

If you are going to get drunk, then YOU must do the drinking! No one else can drink for you! (You have to determine to grab the cup, allow it to be filled, then drink from the cup of God's goodness). There are too many sipping saints in the church! These are the people that only participate in certain activities at certain times or seasons. They just drink on special occasions. We need to be serious drinkers. We need to drink the new wine of the Holy Spirit continually. We need some folks that are so full of the Holy Spirit, they are completely intoxicated, totally under the influence of the Holy Spirit.

Drinking is done with our mouths. It's hard to get drunk if you do not open your mouth. Every time you open your mouth and pray, you are taking a drink. Every time you lift your voice in praise, sing to the Lord, or shout to Him with a voice of triumph, you are taking another drink. You must keep on drinking. You must keep on praying, praising, and lifting your voice to God until you become intoxicated with His presence.

As you are drinking this new wine, out of your belly or innermost being, rivers of living water will begin to flow out of you. These rivers will refresh you and bring life to every area of your life. This is how God intends for us to live our everyday lives. He wants us to continually drink and live under the influence of the Holy Spirit.

The purpose for being filled with the Holy Spirit is found in Acts 1:8 (KJV):

> *But ye shall receive power, after that the Holy Ghost has come upon you: and ye shall be witnesses unto me both in Jerusalem, and in all Judea, and in Samaria, and unto the uttermost part of the earth.*

His purpose is to give us the power to win the lost to Christ!

THE HOLY SPIRIT'S PURPOSE IS TO GIVE US THE POWER TO WIN THE LOST TO CHRIST!

Jesus told His disciples in John 16:7 (KJV) that it was "expedient for you that I go away: for if I go not away, the Comforter will not come unto you; but if I depart, I will send him unto you." Luke 24:49 (KJV) says it like this: "And, behold, I send the promise of my Father upon you: but tarry ye in the city of Jerusalem, until ye be endued with power from on high." The baptism in the Holy Spirit is proof to us that Jesus Christ did ascend into heaven and is now seated at the right hand of our heavenly Father because He told His disciples that He would pray and ask the Father to send the Holy Spirit to them.

In Acts 2, the Holy Spirit made His arrival and filled the believers, and they left the upper room and filled the streets of Jerusalem. These people were carrying the power of the Holy Spirit but also imparting the Holy Spirit to others. Because of this infilling, this small group was able to turn the world upside down for Christ with the great power of the Holy Spirit.

Notice that three thousand souls were added to the church after the first outpouring of the Holy Spirit. Notice that the souls did not come to Christ until the church became intoxicated with the Holy Spirit. Now, our motive for being filled should never be the gifts, manifestations, or even the euphoria of simply being filled. We should not be seeking after manifestations; we should be seeking more of God!

They were intoxicated! They were drunk! They were elated with enthusiasm and happiness! They were delirious with excitement or madness! In other words, they had overdosed on the Holy Spirit. God wants to fill us with the Holy Spirit because He desires to share a relationship with us that is intoxicating, elated with enthusiasm or happiness, delirious with excitement, and continuously overflowing to reach others who need Him!

LET'S TALK ABOUT THE DRUNK MAN
The Drunk Man Cannot Get Enough

He has an unquenchable thirst for this intoxicating Spirit: "If any man thirst, let him come unto me, and drink. He that believeth on me, as the scripture hath said, out of his belly shall flow rivers of living water" (John 7:37-38, KJV) and "Blessed are they which do hunger and thirst for righteousness; for they shall be filled" (Matthew 5:6, KJV). No matter how much a drunk man drinks, he always wants more. Even if he drinks until he passes out, after he wakes up with a horrific hangover, he will still want another drink. (Addicted to drinking.)

God wants us to be so full of the Holy Spirit that we are continuously wanting another drink of His new wine. The person who wants to get drunk does not mind who they drink with; they will drink with anybody that will drink with them. Regardless of who they are or where they come from, what they have or don't have, they just want somebody to drink with them. God wants us to be so full of the Holy Spirit that we are not critical or judgmental toward others. Our desire is just for them to want to drink with us.

The person who wants to get drunk does not wait on someone else to go get them something to drink; they will go get something to drink for themselves. If you will drink with them, they will share their drink with you! We should be actively looking for others who will drink with us.

The Drunk Man Cannot Give Enough

He does not care what it costs him to get drunk; he just wants to get drunk! He's not thinking about how many bills he must pay or the food on his family's table. He just wants to get drunk! You see, he's willing to sacrifice everything he has just to get drunk. I'm here to say that if you get the real wine of the Holy Spirit of the living God, YOU MUST BE WILLING TO PAY THE PRICE—NO MATTER WHAT IT COSTS!

A drunk man is a generous man! If you ask the drunk man for something, he will give it to you. Could it be that the reason so many of us cannot get drunk is that we are not generous with God? Luke 6:38 (KJV) says, "Give, and it shall be given unto you; good measure, pressed down, and shaken together, shall men give into your bosom." And what happened after the Spirit fell in Jerusalem reveals that generosity beautifully:

They continued steadfastly in the apostles' doctrine and fellowship, and in breaking of bread, and in prayers.

And fear came upon every soul: and many wonders and signs were done by the apostles.

And all that believed were together, and had all things common; And sold their possessions and goods, and parted them to all men, as every man had need. And they, continuing daily with one accord in the temple, and breaking bread from house to house, did eat their meat with gladness and singleness of heart, Praising God, and having favor with all the people. And the Lord added to the church daily such as should be saved. Look how generous the people were after they overdosed on the Holy Spirit.
—Acts 2:42–47 (KJV)

The Drunk Man Cannot Be Embarrassed

No matter how silly he sounds, looks, or behaves, he cannot be embarrassed. In the past, true Spirit-filled believers were made fun of, laughed at, and called names. However, you cannot embarrass someone drunk on this new wine! When we are under the influence of the Holy Spirit, we are confident of the power of God that is working in us and not ashamed of what God is doing in us and through us, like Romans 1:16 (KJV): "For I am not ashamed of the gospel of Christ: for it is the power of God unto salvation," describes.

When we are under the influence of the Holy Spirit, there is a holy courage that empowers us to share our testimonies of all that God has done for us without fear or intimidation:

Be not thou therefore ashamed of the testimony of our Lord, nor of me his prisoner: but be thou partaker of the afflictions of the gospel according to the power of God. —2 Timothy 1:8 (KJV)

When we are under the influence of the Holy Spirit, we are not uncomfortable or apprehensive even when we are in the presence of unbelievers and those who live sinful lives:

"Whosoever therefore shall be ashamed of me and of my words in this adulterous and sinful generation; of him also shall the Son of man be ashamed, when he cometh in the glory of his Father with the holy angels." *—Mark 8:38 (KJV)*

When we are under the influence of the Holy Spirit, we are encouraged and empowered to suffer persecution for our faith and endure the discomfort and even heartache and pain that may come because of our commitment to Christ and His kingdom. We are not ashamed of who we are and whom to we belong:

Yet if any man suffer as a Christian, let him not be ashamed; but let him glorify God on this behalf. For the time is come that judgment must begin at the house of God: and if it first begin at us, what shall the end be of them that obey not the gospel of God? And if the righteous scarcely be saved, where shall the ungodly and the sinner appear? Wherefore let them that suffer according to the will of God commit the keeping of their souls to him in well doing, as unto a faithful Creator. —1 Peter 4:16-19 (KJV)

When we live under the influence of the Holy Spirit, we are filled with excitement and expectancy of the soon return of Jesus Christ and not afraid to stand before Him: "And now, little children, abide in him; that, when he shall appear, we may have confidence, and not be ashamed before him at his coming" (1 John 2:28, KJV).

The Drunk Man Loves Everybody

A drunk man loves everybody: his friends, his enemies, strangers, and his family. A drunk man says sweet things. He wants to hug everybody (embrace everyone he meets.) He not only says he loves you with his mouth, but he will prove it with his actions (model the way by what he does and not just what he says. Talk is cheap.). He loves everybody: red, yellow, black, and white they are all precious in His sight. Consider these verses:

- Ephesians 5:1-2 (KJV): "Be ye therefore followers of God, as dear children; And walk in love, as Christ also hath loved us, and hath given himself for us an offering and a sacrifice to God for a sweet-smelling savor."
- John 13:34-35 (KJV): "A new commandment I give unto you, That ye love one another; as I have loved you, that ye also love one another. By this shall all men know that ye are my disciples, if ye have love one to another."
- Romans 12:9-10 (KJV): "Let love be without dissimulation. Abhor that which is evil; cleave to that which is good. Be kindly affectioned one to another with brotherly love; in honour preferring one another."

And there are more: 1 Corinthians 13, Matthew 5:38-48, 1 John 4:7-21, etc.!

The Drunk Man's Song Book

Without a song, you will never survive the hard times.

- Psalm 95:1 (KJV): "O come, let us sing unto the Lord: let us make a joyful noise to the rock of our salvation."
- Psalm 100:1-2 (KJV): "Make a joyful noise unto the Lord, all ye lands. Serve the Lord with gladness: come before his presence with singing."
- Psalm 138:1 (KJV): "I will praise thee with my whole heart: before the gods will I sing praise unto thee."
- Psalm 146:2 (KJV): "While I live will I praise the Lord: I will sing praises unto my God while I have any being."
- Psalm 149:1 (KJV): "Praise ye the Lord. Sing unto the Lord a new song, and his praise in the congregation of saints."
- Ephesians 5:18-19 (KJV): "And be not drunk with wine, wherein is excess; but be filled with the Spirit; Speaking to yourselves in psalms and hymns and spiritual songs, singing and making melody in your heart to the Lord."

In January 2021, my body was severely attacked by the coronavirus. I was in the hospital in the intensive care unit for thirty-two days fighting for my life. My body was almost lifeless since I refused to go on the ventilator. I was unable to even roll myself over in the bed. I lost approximately sixty pounds, and my muscles atrophied. The doctor's reports were negative as they were not giving very much hope that I would recover. Many others in the hospital were dying; it was a very discouraging and depressing situation to be in.

I can remember over and over again, waking up with songs running through my heart. Often, they were songs I had heard in the church. Others were songs my wife and daughters loved to sing. Still others were songs I knew and loved. And sometimes, it was lyric and tune I had never heard before. All the while my body was ravaged with the virus, my lungs were under severe attack, and I was fighting for every breath, inside, I was singing, singing, singing! My spirit was filled with songs of thanks, of praise to my God. My heart was overflowing with worship with every breath. My body was very sick, but my spirit was under the influence of the Holy Spirit and worshiping, worshiping, worshiping!

You must have a song from the Lord! The Holy Spirit is a Spirit of joy! Not just in the good times but especially in the difficult and discouraging times. This is much stronger and more powerful than happiness. Happiness is a hypocrite. Happiness will leave you when the house burns down, but, God's joy will hang around and sit with you in the ashes, get up with you, and help you rebuild. Happiness will leave you when discouragement comes, but God's joy will hang around and help you fight off the discouraging spirits that try to torment you. Drink until the joy of the Holy Spirit is overflowing in you. Live in the overflowing joy that comes from your relationship with God.

He is waiting on you today to acknowledge His presence and include Him in everything, at all times, in all places, and with everyone else. He wants to be included and involved in every area and affair of your life. He wants you to be drenched in His presence! Drink of God's presence until you're like a drunk person, and everything in you will be affected: the way you see, hear, speak, and walk out every day.

Pray with me:

Hello, Holy Spirit. Thank You so much for Your presence in my life. I want to be in constant fellowship and friendship with You. I'm asking You to assist and advise me in everything and with everyone in my life. In Jesus's name, I pray. Amen.

CHAPTER 4

SUPER FRUITFUL

LIVING YOUR BEST LIFE IN THIS WORLD

T his continuous drenching that causes you to overflow with supernatural hope, faith, and love is empowering you to live a life that affects everyone around you. Sometimes, even in the church, people have been turned off from seeking for this continuous drenching by people who profess to be Spirit-filled and yet do not have the character and attitudes of Christ manifesting in their lives.

This drenching is meant to develop in you the nature, character, and attitudes of Christ. It is meant to make you victorious over every obstacle, challenge, battle, and attack you will face in this life—and sometimes the biggest enemy is us. This drenching is meant to help us overcome ourselves and all our selfish, childish, and foolish desires and ways. As we begin to mature in this drenching, others around us are going to be influenced by the victory we are experiencing.

We are living in a constant war zone. There is a war going on inside of every born-again believer. According to Galatians 5, our flesh or carnal human nature is in constant battle with the Holy

Spirit living in us. These two forces living in us are continuously opposing one another. We are going to give in to one or the other. We must train ourselves to give in to the Holy Spirit living in us:

> *So I say, let the Holy Spirit guide your lives. Then you won't be doing what your sinful nature craves. The sinful nature wants to do evil, which is just the opposite of what the Spirit wants. And the Spirit gives us desires that are the opposite of what the sinful nature desires. These two forces are constantly fighting each other, so you are not free to carry out your good intentions. But when you are directed by the Spirit, you are not under obligation to the law of Moses. When you follow the desires of your sinful nature, the results are very clear: sexual immorality, impurity, lustful pleasures, idolatry, sorcery, hostility, quarreling, jealousy, outbursts of anger, selfish ambition, dissension, division, envy, drunkenness, wild parties, and other sins like these. Let me tell you again, as I have before, that anyone living that sort of life will not inherit the Kingdom of God.*
>
> *But the Holy Spirit produces this kind of fruit in our lives: love, joy, peace, patience, kindness, goodness, faithfulness, gentleness, and self-control. There is no law against these things!*
>
> *Those who belong to Christ Jesus have nailed the passions and desires of their sinful nature to his cross and crucified them there. Since we are living by the Spirit, let us follow the Spirit's leading in every part of our lives.*
> —Galatians 5:16-25 (NLT)

Without the Holy Spirit, we are powerless against our fleshly desires and selfishness. We need a force greater than ourselves to overcome ourselves. On our own, no matter how much we desire, we cannot produce the good works and fruitfulness of God.

God wants us to be full of the fruit of the Holy Spirit. However, we cannot produce it for ourselves. We can modify our behavior, conduct, and even our conversation, but we cannot produce the fruit of the Holy Spirit. The fruit of the Holy Spirit is not natural fruit. It cannot be produced in us by any kind of natural means. The fruit of the Holy Spirit is supernatural fruit and can only be produced in us by the Holy Spirit, who is the supernatural power of God living in us.

When the apostle Paul writes in Galatians 5 about the "fruit," he is trying to help us understand what the Holy Spirit is trying to produce in us as we acknowledge and yield ourselves to him every day. The Holy Spirit in us is in a continuous process of producing supernatural love, joy, peace, patience, kindness, goodness, faithfulness, gentleness, and self-control.

THE FRUIT OF THE SPIRIT IS PRODUCED BY THE HOLY SPIRIT, NOT BY THE BELIEVER.

Notice the word *fruit* is singular—not plural—showing us that the fruit is a unified whole, not independent characteristics. However, as we grow in our relationship with the Holy Spirit, all the characteristics of Christ will be manifested in us.

Just like physical fruit needs time to grow, the fruit of the Spirit also needs time to grow and develop. The fruit of the Spirit does not ripen overnight, and just like a successful farmer or gardener must battle against weeds to enjoy the sweet fruit they desire, we must constantly work to rid ourselves of the weeds of our old sinful nature that want to choke out the word of God.

The Holy Spirit gives us the power we need to reject the old sinful desires. We can say no to sin and accept the way out that God faithfully provides (see 1 Corinthians 10:13) by following the directions of the Holy Spirit. And as we give the Holy Spirit more control of our lives, He begins to do in and through us what only He can do—grow and develop us to be like Jesus (see 2 Corinthians 3:17-18).

Since God's desire for all His children is for us to be like Jesus (see Romans 8:29), the Holy Spirit constantly works to rid us of the acts of our sinful nature (see Galatians 5:19) and display His fruit instead. Therefore, the presence of the fruit of the Spirit is evidence that our character is becoming more like Christ's. Paul uses nine characteristics to describe the fruit of the Spirit in Galatians 5.

THE FRUIT
Love

True, biblical love at its highest level is a choice, not a feeling. This love deliberately chooses to express itself in caring ways and always has the best interests of others at heart and in mind. This love is dependent on the character of Christ, not feelings or emotions. This love chooses to set aside one's own preferences and desires, and, sometimes, even needs to put the other person first (see Philippians 2:1-3). We may need to ask ourselves, *Am I more concerned about my reputation or with the edification of others around me that need the love that only God can give?*

Joy

As believers, if we are not careful, we can downplay the meaning of joy. As we cling tightly to Jesus, abiding daily in our saving relationship with Him, we will experience the fullness of the kind of joy Jesus promised (see John 15:4-11). Sometimes, we may need to ask ourselves, *Am I bringing joy-filled encouragement to the other people in my life?*

Peace

The world doesn't offer very much peace. Just look around. The world cannot give this peace because the world doesn't know the One who is peace. But for those who have the Spirit of peace within, the peace of Christ is possible, no matter our circumstances (see John 14:27). We can reject the chaos of the world and embrace God's peace. The book of Philippians tells us how (see Philippians 4:4-9).

- Choose to rejoice in God and who He is.
- Bring all your worries, fears, and concerns to God in prayer.
- Fill your mind with God's truth.
- Choose to think about the things of God.

Sometimes, we may need to ask ourselves, *Am I doing all I can to promote peace in the church and in the lives of the others around me?*

Patience

We don't see much patience in the world today, either—not even like we need to in the church. Maybe part of the reason is our fast-paced, want-it-now culture. But born-again believers have everything we need to be patient because we have the Holy Spirit living in us and longing to display His character to those around us. Patient people put up with circumstances and other people, even when severely tested and tried. They display endurance, longsuffering, and perseverance.

The New Testament also specifically connects patience with sharing the gospel. God is patient as He waits for the lost to come to Him (see 2 Peter 3:9), and He calls His people to be patient as we work to lead others to their own salvation in Christ (see 2 Timothy 4:20). Sometimes, we may need to ask ourselves, *Is it the right time to say this, or should I wait until later when I may be thinking more clearly and less reactively?*

Kindness and Goodness

The characteristics of kindness and goodness are closely related. Together, they present the picture of one who not only possesses moral goodness and integrity but also generously expresses it in the way they act toward others. This goodness in action reflects God's kindness and goodness toward us. God demonstrated His kindness and goodness to us in our salvation (see Titus 3:4) and will continue to "show the immeasurable riches of His grace in kindness toward us" for all eternity (Ephesians 2:7, ESV). Sometimes, we may need to ask ourselves, *Are my words and actions kind?*

Faithfulness

To be faithful is to be reliable or trustworthy. For every born-again believer, this is faithfulness specifically to Jesus Christ, who has redeemed us by His precious blood. For born-again believers, faithfulness is the continued and consistent submission and obedience to the same Spirit who provides us with the ability to be faithful. This attitude is in direct contrast to our previous faithfulness to our own sinful desires and ways.

The word also describes someone who is willing to suffer persecution and even death for Christ's sake: "Therefore, among God's churches we boast about your perseverance and faith in all the persecutions and trials you are enduring" (2 Thessalonians 1:4, NIV). Sometimes we may need to ask ourselves, *Am I attempting to say or do something that will cause people to trust in Jesus or applaud me?*

Gentleness and Meekness

Closely linked to humility, gentleness is grace of the soul. It is not weakness, but instead, it is strength under control. For instance, in Paul's second letter to Timothy, he wrote that the Lord's servant will correct his opponents with gentleness (see 2 Timothy 2:25). And in his letter to the church in Galatia, he wrote that those who have been caught in sin should be restored in a spirit of gentleness (see Galatians 6:1, XXX). Gentleness, is the opposite of self-assertiveness and self-interest and is also the key ingredient to unity and peace within the body of Christ (see Ephesians 4:2). Sometimes, we may need to ask ourselves, *Am I speaking more harshly than needed simply because I want to make an example of those who may disagree with me?*

Self-Control

The last characteristic in Paul's description of the fruit of the Spirit points back to his list of the works of the flesh in

Galatians 5:19-21. Those of us with the indwelling Holy Spirit have the strength to control our sinful desires and to say no to our flesh. Self-control gives us the power to say yes to the Spirit, which allows Him to produce in us a beautiful and bountiful harvest of supernatural spiritual fruit. Sometimes we may need to ask ourselves, *Should I actually say or do this?* Or, *Is this better left unsaid or undone?*

For the Holy Spirit to produce His super-fruit, we must submit every area to the Holy Spirit—maybe even asking ourselves these questions when we are interacting on social media and the internet. Does your social media feed and internet activity display the super-fruit of the Holy Spirit?

God and Jesus Christ command and expect us to bear good fruit—and not just any ordinary fruit, but the fruit of the Holy Spirit. We know that the fruit is produced by the Holy Spirit. That is why it is called the fruit of the Holy Spirit and not the fruit of ourselves. On our own, we are only capable of producing the works of the flesh. Although we can modify our behavior, conduct, and conversation, and produce to some degree some of the reflections of the fruit of the Holy Spirit, it will never be enough.

When others see us allowing the Holy Spirit to produce His super-fruit in us, it also produces a genuine credibility with others that causes them to have great confidence in the God we serve and believe that He can also produce good things in their lives. This drenching is ongoing, and as we continue to allow the Holy Spirit to produce His supernatural fruit in us, we will develop credibility with Him, and He will continue to lead us into greater levels of His power in our lives. So, get ready; you have not received all that God has for you yet. There is more on the way.

Pray with me:

Dear heavenly Father, thank You so much for sending the Holy Spirit into my life. Holy Spirit, I'm asking You to work in my life and produce Your fruit. I'm asking You to develop Your character in me so that others will have confidence in You because of Your fruit they see in my life. In Jesus's name, I pray. Amen.

CHAPTER 5

SUPERNATURAL LANGUAGES AND OTHER GIFTS

LIVING BEYOND YOUR OWN ABILITIES

A s you continue to walk with the Holy Spirit and enjoy His daily fellowship, you will develop a closer relationship with Him and begin to take on His characteristics. As you continue to cooperate and participate with the Holy Spirit, He will produce His fruit. And, like rain falling down from heaven, this baptism in the Holy Spirit or drenching (thoroughly covered and completely filled with His presence) will produce in you a burning desire to have all that God has to offer you. As you allow this heavenly rain to fall on you, the Holy Spirit will begin to display His supernatural gifts in you. God has promised many gifts to every believer who will believe and receive all that He has to offer them.

As you are drenched in His presence, the first gift every believer will receive is the gift of spiritual languages, like in Mark 16:17 (KJV): "They shall speak with new tongues." God gives every Spirit-filled or drenched believer their own spiritual language.

This is not something we should resist or question but joyfully and willfully receive.

A SPIRITUAL LANGUAGE IS OUR BLESSING FROM OUR HEAVENLY FATHER AND OUR SOURCE OF SPIRITUAL POWER FOR EVERYDAY LIVING.

The apostle Paul said, "I thank my God, I speak with tongues more than you all" (1 Corinthians 14:18, KJV). Speaking in spiritual languages was something that the apostle Paul practiced daily. If the apostle Paul found it necessary to practice speaking in spiritual languages daily in his time here, we most definitely need to practice speaking in spiritual languages daily while we are here. Spiritual languages are a blessing from our heavenly Father and our source of Spiritual power for everyday living.

When you begin to speak in a spiritual language as the Holy Spirit gives you the ability to do, this is the initial sign that you have been baptized in the Holy Spirit or drenched—thoroughly covered and completely filled with the presence of God. It's like Acts 2:4 (KJV): "They were all filled with the Holy Ghost and began to speak with other tongues, as the Spirit gave them the utterance."

This spiritual language you receive is the supernatural evidence of the Holy Spirit living in you and empowering you to serve Him and do incredible exploits for the glory of God, the encouragement of His church, and especially to be a witness to others of the power of the gospel of Christ everywhere you are.

Many believers refer to this spiritual language as a "prayer language" because, many times, this spiritual language comes during times of prayer and worship. There are also many benefits and advantages this drenching brings. Allowing this spiritual language to speak through us, encourages us and gives us a tremendous advantage over the discouragements and depressions that come with living in this fallen and broken world. First Corinthians 14:4 (KJV, clarification added) says, "He that speaks in an unknown tongue edifieth [encourages and builds up] himself."

Notice this is called an *unknown tongue,* meaning there is no other language like your spiritual language in the Earth. It is not a language spoken by anyone on the Earth. This is a great advantage because it means no one, human or demonic, can understand what is being said. This language is only understood by God Himself. It may not come with any interpretation because it is most likely unnecessary since it is a language being spoken between you and your heavenly Father. Private between you and your heavenly Father, it doesn't include others in the conversation. It is for your daily encouragement and refreshing.

When you are speaking in this spiritual language, you are personally being refreshed and recharged or energized to continue blessing and encouraging others, like in 1 Corinthians 14:2 (KJV): "For he that speaks in an unknown tongue speaks not unto men, but unto God: for no man understands him, howbeit in the Spirit he speaks mysteries." This also means the Holy Spirit speaks divine secrets in direct communication with God Himself.

When you allow this spiritual language to operate through you, you will be reminded that the Holy Spirit with all His power and presence is empowering you:

> *And I will ask the Father, and he will give you another advocate to help you and be with you forever—the Spirit of truth. The world cannot accept him because it neither sees him nor knows him. But you know him, for he lives with you and will be in you. —John 14:16-17 (NIV)*

This drenching is a supernatural empowering intended for us to experience for the rest of our lives. It is meant to develop spiritual gifts in us and to help us overcome the weaknesses we have.

THIS DRENCHING IS A SUPERNATURAL EMPOWERING INTENDED FOR US TO EXPERIENCE FOR THE REST OF OUR LIVES. IT IS MEANT TO DEVELOP SPIRITUAL GIFTS IN US AND TO HELP US OVERCOME THE WEAKNESSES WE HAVE.

Another incredible benefit of allowing spiritual languages to operate in us is that when we are praying in these unknown languages we are always praying in the perfect will of God:

> *Likewise the Spirit also helpeth our infirmities: for we know not what we should pray for as we ought: but the*

Spirit itself maketh intercession for us with groanings which cannot be uttered. And he that searcheth the hearts knoweth what is the mind of the Spirit because he maketh intercession for the saints according to the will of God.
—Romans 8:26-27 (KJV)

When we are praying in our spiritual language, the Holy Spirit Himself is praying through us. Praying in spiritual languages keeps selfishness out of our prayers. Praying in spiritual languages strengthens and stimulates our faith: "But ye, beloved, building up yourselves on your most holy faith, praying in the Holy Ghost" (Jude 20, KJV). It helps us to trust God with greater confidence in His abilities.

We are living in a fallen and broken world. A world filled with temptation and out of control with the lusts of the flesh, the lust of the eyes, and the pride of life, and without this drenching, it is very easy to be influenced by the world and drawn back into sinful lives and lifestyles. This drenching empowers us to be in this world but not of it. In other words, the Holy Spirit helps us to not compromise our character and live separated from this broken and present world.

Praying in our spiritual language causes us to pray for the unknown. The Holy Spirit knows everything and searches all hearts and minds; therefore, He helps us pray for things we are not even aware of.

Praying in our spiritual language brings spiritual rest and refreshing, like it says in Isaiah 28:11-12 (KJV): "For with stammering lips and another tongue will he speak to this people. To whom he said, This is the rest wherewith ye may cause the weary to rest; and this is the refreshing." This can happen to us on a daily basis, if we will allow the spiritual language of the Holy Spirit to operate in us on a daily basis.

Notice how the initial evidence of speaking in spiritual languages is to be used privately and publicly with proper respect and order for everyone that may be affected:

> So what shall I do? I will pray with my spirit, but I will also pray with my understanding; I will sing with my spirit, but I will also sing with my understanding. Otherwise when you are praising God in the Spirit, how can someone else, who is now put in the position of an inquirer, say "Amen" to your thanksgiving, since they do not know what you are saying? You are giving thanks well enough, but no one else is edified. —1 Corinthians 14:15-17 (NIV)

Paul says that when you are in the presence of others, don't speak in spiritual languages all the time, but also speak with a language others can understand. Notice he is not forbidding speaking in spiritual languages in public, but he is saying also speak in languages that others can understand. Maybe one of the most necessary benefits of speaking in spiritual languages is it requires us to bring our tongues under subjection to the Holy Spirit and helps us to completely yield our tongue to the will of God. This is necessary since James 5:8 (KJV) says, "But the tongue can no man tame, it is an unruly evil, full of deadly poison. This is an incredible step in yielding our whole body to God." If we can give the tongue, we can give the rest of our bodies since our tongues seem to be the most difficult part to surrender and bring under subjection. Perhaps this is a major reason God has chosen the speaking in tongues as a sign of the baptism in the Holy Spirit.

Now, this gift of spiritual languages has been misunderstood and abused in many ways that have caused some believers to resist this drenching. I want to share with you something amazing and comforting about receiving this special gift. The Holy Spirit is a perfect gentleman. He will not force Himself on you or force you to do something you are not willing to do.

We know the Holy Spirit is a person. He lives inside of us, so let's answer some questions about how the Holy Spirit works in us.

THE PRESSING QUESTIONS

What does the Holy Spirit do in your life, and what qualities do you receive from Him?

1) The Holy Spirit is a gift and the giver of gifts.

Each of us was created by God with natural gifts that must be discovered and developed over the course of our lives. The Holy Spirit puts supernatural gifts inside of us that He chooses and develops for His purposes and for the building up of the church. First Corinthians 12:4-5, 8-9 (KJV) describes this: "Now there are diversities of gifts, but the same Spirit. And there are differences of administrations, but the same Lord. . . . For to one is given by the Spirit the word of Wisdom, to another the word of Knowledge by the same Spirit, to another Faith by the same Spirit, to another the gifts of healing by the same Spirit." The Holy Spirit decides what gifts you receive.

2) The Holy Spirit can provide you a prayer language that nobody understands but God.

Your prayer language is a precious and important gift. Praying in a heavenly language (tongues) is an incredible phenomenon, and a relationship with us is essential in the world of our Creator the Holy Spirit. He provided every nationality a language of its own, and the Holy Spirit has a language. Here are some things you should know about tongues and your prayer language. This is powerful because not even Satan can understand your prayer language; it's a direct line to our heavenly Father by the Holy Spirit who intercedes for us.

OUR PRAYER LANGUAGE IS A DIRECT LINE TO OUR HEAVENLY FATHER BY THE HOLY SPIRIT WHO INTERCEDES FOR US.

3) **When you pray in the Holy Spirit, trust Him enough to avoid logic and the temptation to understand everything He is doing.**

Trust the Holy Spirit, and do not try to figure out what He is trying to say unless you feel like there must be an interpretation. Then you may ask the Holy Spirit to interpret what He just said. Trust Him; He is at work.

4) **It is important for you to keep your prayer language alive and vibrant.**

The apostle Paul in 1 Corinthians 14:18 (KJV) says, "I thank my God, I speak with tongues more than you all." The Holy Spirit is interceding on your behalf to the heavenly Father, so it's important for you to pray in your prayer language every day so that the Holy Spirit can reveal wisdom and help you as you progress. Your prayer language can be used any time you pray: in your secret place, in your car, in your home, at church, etc.

If you have been filled with the Holy Spirit but are not using your prayer language daily, then ask your heavenly Father for your prayer language. You can ask anything in the name of Jesus, and your Father in heaven will do it for you. We know that it is God's will for you to receive because Jesus said in Luke 11:13 (KJV) "If you then, being evil, know how to give good gifts to your children, how much more will your heavenly Father give the Holy Spirit to them that ask Him."

5) Does the Holy Spirit have His own native tongue?

The Holy Spirit knows every language in the universe. All languages—known and unknown—are native to Him. By known, I mean there is someone human who understands. Unknown means that only God the Father, God the Son, and God the Holy Spirit understand.

6) How can some people just start speaking in tongues, but others, when they pray, take a long time?

For the person who has received the baptism of the Holy Spirit with the evidence of speaking in tongues as the Spirit gives the utterance, it is a matter of yielding yourself to the person of the Holy Spirit living inside you.

The Bible teaches that the Spirit is subject to the person He is living in. He will not speak if you do not allow Him to speak through you. He is ready to speak and pray through you the instant you yield and allow your heavenly language to flow unless there are hindrances such as unconfessed, hidden, or secret sins or anything else that could grieve or quench the Holy Spirit.

The Holy Spirit is like a dove, very gentle and easily disturbed. Therefore, it's important that we keep clean from sin before God and spend much time in God's presence through thanksgiving, praise, worship, and prayer to make us sensitive to the Holy Spirit living in us, so that we may sense His leading, prompting, and guidance daily. This language, your heavenly prayer language, is with you continuously, day and night. The Holy Spirit only needs you to recognize, acknowledge, and give in to Him and His leadership.

You may pray in the Spirit in private and in public. In public, you may pray in your heavenly language under your breath so as not to draw attention to yourself but to allow the Holy Spirit His freedom to direct you. You may sing in your heavenly language in your private/public worship. Allow the Holy Spirit to worship through you, exalting Jesus Christ but never drawing attention to yourself and being overzealous with distracting or disturbing demonstrations.

For the Holy Spirit to have the freedom He needs to operate in us as He wills, we must diligently line our lives up with the written Word of God, making a complete, whole-hearted commitment and dedication to live for Jesus Christ. We must be His representative on the Earth as a witness of His death, burial, resurrection, and the change He has made in our lives. Allow the Holy Spirit to daily search our hearts and minds for anything that may be displeasing to God, asking God to create within us clean hearts and pure minds.

Many times, there are hindrances in us that grieve and quench the Holy Spirit's freedom to operate and flow. Therefore, we must daily surrender ourselves and submit ourselves to God's Word and His will. Most importantly, we must admit the Holy Spirit is with us and within us and yield to and give in to Him and His ways with our minds, spirits, and bodies, allowing His thoughts, will, and ways to flow through us, that He may use us as He pleases. As He speaks into our minds and spirits, we use our bodies to express His thoughts, will, ways, and language.

He is the ultimate gentleman and will never force Himself upon anyone. He will never take from you your ability to control your mental, emotional, spiritual, or physical faculties. If the heavenly language flows through you, it will be you who speaks, your voice that is heard, and your tongue and lips that form the words. The Holy Spirit will give you the utterances, but He will not speak them for you. You must yield and speak forth the utterances as He gives them.

~~~~~~~~~~~~~~~~~~

THE HOLY SPIRIT WILL GIVE YOU THE UTTERANCES, BUT HE WILL NOT SPEAK THEM FOR YOU. YOU MUST YIELD AND SPEAK FORTH THE WORDS AS HE GIVES THEM.

~~~~~~~~~~~~~~~~~~

7) Why do people laugh in the Spirit or fall down when the Holy Spirit moves on and in them?

The Holy Spirit is a supernatural phenomenon from the supernatural world. Therefore, the natural mind, spirit, and body cannot adequately and sufficiently contain the abundance of supernatural energy that is filling, flowing through, and overflowing from them. It is a supernatural experience that requires supernatural evidence, and there may be many and various manifestations in the natural realm.

The Holy Spirit can but is not limited to manifestations that include language, the quickening of our mortal bodies, trances, healings, miracles, prophecies, words in known or unknown languages, interpretations of languages, the ability to discern spirits, wisdom, and knowledge. The Holy Spirit could possibly manifest Himself with a special touch of His presence upon someone to speak the Word of God, sing, worship, skillfully play instruments, pray and intercede, or even impart special abilities to use natural skills and talents. The Holy Spirit is unlimited in His scope and ability to manifest Himself through anyone with any of their natural abilities or any of His supernatural abilities. One may dance, spin, fall prostrate, shout loudly, weep, or laugh with joy as they allow the Holy Spirit to flow and overflow through their bodies.

The Holy Spirit can reveal Himself by giving us dreams and visions, as well. He can speak to us about our past, present, and future. There is no limit to the Holy Spirit's ability, ways of manifesting and revealing Himself, and His will to us. The overall key factor is that every manifestation and revelation be for the absolute and distinct purpose of exalting and drawing attention to Jesus Christ. Manifestations, especially of the physical or natural kind, should *never* be for the purpose of drawing attention to ourselves, distracting others, or any kind of fleshly display for the sake of appearing strange, weird, or spooky.

The Holy Spirit may use you to speak in known or unknown languages, prophesy, give special words of wisdom or knowledge, and maybe interpret a language. Never add to or take from any of the messages the Holy Spirit may give you; speak only as you are moved or prompted without excuse or explanation. Simply be obedient to the Holy Spirit. All manifestations of the Holy Spirit are directed at His will and not our own. We are never to manufacture a manifestation. The Holy Spirit chooses how He desires to manifest Himself.

There may be ways other than these that the Holy Spirit uses. God's ways are so much higher than our ways, so we can never limit the Holy Spirit to any expression we have already experienced or witnessed others experience. We must simply be obedient to the moving and the promptings of the Holy Spirit living in us.

8) How do you know when the Holy Spirit is moving in you and you are not just excited or hyped up?

Your relationship with the Holy Spirit is one of daily learning and growing, most importantly through reading, meditating, memorizing, and learning the written Word of God. The more you read and learn the Holy Scripture, the more you will grow and mature in your understanding of how the Holy Spirit affects you emotionally. We are emotional creatures, and we must always prevent our emotions from overtaking and leading us into fleshly demonstrations.

Emotionally, we may cry, laugh, or shout. We may bow, lie, fall down, jump, leap, dance, or respond emotionally in other ways. We must develop a spiritual discipline to keep our emotions in submission to the Holy Spirit at all times. We must not allow ourselves to get into fanaticism, religious legalism, or spiritual/emotional/physical excesses, thus distracting and taking away from the true purpose and intention of any manifestation the Holy Spirit may demonstrate or display through us. You always want your emotional response to be authentic and genuine, not merely emotional or physical exercise or excitement. Although many times a manifestation of the Holy Spirit will be an extremely emotional and exciting experience, what we must always remember is that the manifestation is not for the purpose of thrilling us emotionally but for exalting Jesus Christ.

BEING DRENCHED IN THE HOLY SPIRIT WILL BE THE MOST EXCITING, INCREDIBLE, AND POWERFUL RELATIONSHIP YOU WILL EVER EXPERIENCE AND ENJOY THIS SIDE OF HEAVEN.

Being drenched in the Holy Spirit will be the most exciting, incredible, and powerful relationship you will ever experience and enjoy this side of heaven. As you experience the amazing gifts of the Holy Spirit, and you allow your spiritual language to flow daily, prepare yourself to go deeper and more intimate in your prayer life.

Pray with me:

Lord Jesus, I ask You now to baptize me in the Holy Spirit. Holy Spirit, I'm asking You to give me the utterances of spiritual languages. As they come, I'm asking You to give me the courage to speak them and allow them to flow freely through me as You make intercession to my heavenly Father. In Jesus's name, I pray. Amen.

CHAPTER 6

THE SECRET CODE

HIS INTERCESSION

As we continue to grow in allowing the supernatural gifts of the Holy Spirit to operate, we will discover that every time His gifts are active in us, it's like being drenched over and over again—especially the gift of tongues, which we refer to as the unknown language or our personal prayer language. As we allow the Holy Spirit to pray through us, we begin to understand that it is like a secret code between us and our heavenly Father—a secret code that no one understands, especially not Satan or any of his demons. This secret code causes us to pray in the perfect will of God and causes our prayers to be much more powerful and effective. This secret code is the secret to the power of prayer. This is especially effective when we don't know how to pray. When we allow the Holy Spirit to pray, He always knows exactly what to say to our heavenly Father on our behalf.

The Holy Spirit is our prayer partner to help us pray effectively. We may have prayer partners and prayer groups, but the greatest prayer partner is the Holy Spirit. What a concept that the Holy Spirit partners with us to pray! The greatest privilege that God has given to us is the freedom to approach Him at any time. We are not only authorized to speak to Him but we are invited. Not only are we permitted, but we are also expected to speak to God. God waits for us to communicate with Him. We have instant, direct access to God. However, in these bodies of flesh, there are times when we cannot communicate with God as we should.

WHEN WE ALLOW THE HOLY SPIRIT TO PRAY, HE ALWAYS KNOWS EXACTLY WHAT TO SAY TO OUR HEAVENLY FATHER ON OUR BEHALF.

So God sent us the Holy Spirit, who dwells within every born-again believer, and one of His functions is to help us in our prayer life. We find this truth in Romans 8:26-28 (NIV):

Likewise the Spirit also helps in our weaknesses. For we do not know what we should pray for as we ought, but the Spirit Himself makes intercession for us with groanings which cannot be uttered. Now He who searches the hearts knows what the mind of the Spirit is because He makes intercession for the saints according to the will of God. And we know that all things work together for good to those who love God, to those who are called according to His purpose.

There are several truths I want to share with you.

THE HOLY SPIRIT INTERCEDES WITH US

This truth is good news. How many times have you said or thought, *I don't know what to say when I pray?* You have gone to God in prayer, and when you tried to pray, the burden was so great, or the problem was so heavy, you didn't even know where to begin? You see, what God has given to us is not just a book of instructions on how to pray. He has given us a person, Someone who will pray with us and for us—the Holy Spirit.

The word intercession in verse 26 is not the same Greek word in verse 27. In verse 26, the word means that the Holy Spirit goes WITH us to the Father to help plead for our needs. The truth is that we are finite beings, and we have, as this verse says, weaknesses. Therefore, there are times when we do not know what to pray for.

This is how it works:

1) I go to prayer, but I don't know what I need or what to pray for.

2) The Holy Spirit DOES know what I need.

3) As I pray, the Holy Spirit shows me my needs.

4) I then take my needs to the Father, and He—the Holy Spirit—goes with me to the Father.

So, I go to my knees in prayer, and I cry to the Holy Spirit, saying, *Oh, Holy Spirit, I don't know what I need today. I don't know what God's will is in this matter. Holy Spirit, will you help me and show me what I need today?* And He does; then, the Holy Spirit goes with me to the Father. He knows the Father better than I do, so what better person could I have to go with me to the Father when I present my needs and petitions than the Holy Spirit who has led me in making my petitions?

Let me try to help us understand this by sharing some other verses with you. Ephesians 2:18 (NIV) says, "For through Him we both have access by one Spirit to the Father." Now, notice the word both. The way prayer works is like this: we pray to the Father, through the Son, with the Holy Spirit. Our access to the Father is through His Son. Our prayer partner when we go to the Father is the Holy Spirit.

Now look at Acts 15:28 (NIV): "For it seemed good to the Holy Spirit and to us, to lay upon you no greater burden than these necessary things." Oh, I like those words: it seemed good to the Holy Spirit AND TO US. Notice the agreement there. There was a fellowship between the Holy Spirit and the apostles. They had communed with the Holy Spirit. They had been with Him to the Father. We are not to just fall on our knees and start telling God what we want and what we need. No! We go to the Holy Spirit, who impresses upon us what we really need. He leads us as we go to the Father; we go to the Father, and the Holy Spirit accompanies us.

He leads me as I talk to the Father, also talking personally with the Father and confirming my petitions. There is a way that the Christian can walk in the Spirit, with the Spirit, and through the Spirit until God's wants become our wants and His desires become our desires. His delights become our delights. His will becomes our will. Oh, what a joy it is to have the Holy Spirit intercede with us!

THE HOLY SPIRIT INTERCEDES FOR US

Did you know that if we only received from God what we asked for, we would not get everything that we needed? But the verse says that even when we don't know what to pray for, the Spirit makes intercession for us. Intercession here does not imply the Holy Spirit meeting with us to plead. This is the Holy Spirit coming before God for us, on our behalf. Here, He tells God about the needs that I have forgotten to ask for,\ or did not even know that I had. You see, He is now interceding FOR me, where, before, He was interceding WITH me. The Holy Spirit, who is faithful, intercedes FOR me, making sure that I get the things that will work together for my good.

EVEN WHEN WE DON'T KNOW WHAT TO PRAY FOR, THE SPIRIT MAKES INTERCESSION FOR US.

Some of these may not be the things I would choose myself, but He knows what I need, so He intercedes before the Father on my behalf, asking the Father to give me things that I NEED.

I may want the sun to shine every day, but He may know that I need a cloudy day.

I may want all noontime, but He may know that I need midnight.

I may want all mountaintops, but He may know that I need a valley.

I may want all smiles, but He may know that I need tears.

I like to illustrate it this way: At Christmas time, a child asks for things that they want but not always what they need. A loving father, along with the toys, games, and fun, will buy also what their child needs. So along with the new doll, is a pair of boots, or along with the new bike, is a sweater or a warm jacket. Why? Because those are things the earthly father knows will work together for their child's good.

This is where Romans 8:28 comes in: "And we know that all things work together for good to them that love God, to them who are the called according to His purpose." I heard a minister tell about a man years ago in a tent meeting in Florida. After the service, a preacher and an old man were kneeling at the altar praying. The old man with a tear-stained face, looked toward heaven, and prayed, "Dear Lord, I hate baking powder. Dear Lord, I hate flour. Dear Lord, I hate salt. Dear Lord, I hate shortening." He prayed on, listing several other things, and then a smile came across his face, and He prayed, "Dear Lord, put those things all together, stir them up, and put them in the oven, and I sure do like golden brown biscuits."

That is the joy of having the Holy Spirit as an intercessor. He knows what I need, what is for my good, and He intercedes for me.

THE HOLY SPIRIT INCREASES OUR DESIRE TO PRAY

Just as it is natural for a child to talk to their earthly father, so it is just as natural for a believer to want to talk to their heavenly Father. The Holy Spirit living inside us encourages and increases our desire to pray. It is a sure sign of spiritual sickness when we lack a desire to pray. A carnal Christian will find many excuses why they don't have time to pray.

Let me tell you that Satan is always ready to try to rob us of our time alone with God because he knows it is our source of strength, but when the Holy Spirit is indwelling us and filling us, He will draw us to the place of prayer, so we can talk with our heavenly Father. We find this in the life of Christ Himself.

THE HOLY SPIRIT LIVING INSIDE US ENCOURAGES AND INCREASES OUR DESIRE TO PRAY.

Look at what it says in Luke 4:1 (NIV): "Then Jesus, being filled with the Holy Spirit, returned from the Jordan and was led by the Spirit into the wilderness." And we know that it was there that He fasted and prayed and, afterward, was tempted by the devil, but it was the Holy Spirit who drew him to the place of prayer. And when the Holy Spirit is dwelling in us and filling us, He will give us the desire to commune with our heavenly Father.

THROUGH PRAYER, THE HOLY SPIRIT OPENS OUR EYES TO THE NEEDS AROUND US

It is through prayer that the Holy Spirit can give us insight into what others may fail to see. He can help us see where God wants to move and work. He can inspire us to pray for a person or a situation that we would never have even been aware of if it weren't for the Holy Spirit bringing those needs to us as we pray.

We find this truth in Act 10. In verse 9, Peter went up to the rooftop to pray while he was waiting for the evening meal to get ready, and the Holy Spirit showed him that he should no longer call the Gentiles unclean. Then in verse 30, Cornelius was praying and fasting, asking for God's direction in his life, and the Holy Spirit, through prayer, told him to go to a certain town and to a certain house in that town and ask for a man by the name of Peter.

Jeremiah 33:3 (NIV) tells us, "Call to Me, and I will answer you, and show you great and mighty things, which you do not know." It is the Holy Spirit who brings needs and insights to our attention. When Jesus Christ faced the greatest crisis of His life—the cross—He felt the need for prayer. We find this in Matthew 26:

> *Then Jesus came with them to a place called Gethsemane, and said to the disciples, "Sit here while I go and pray over there." And He took with Him Peter and the two sons of Zebedee, and He began to be sorrowful and deeply distressed. Then He said to them, "My soul is exceedingly sorrowful, even to death. Stay here and watch with Me." He went a little farther and fell on His face, and prayed, saying, "O My Father, if it is possible, let this cup pass from Me; nevertheless, not as I will, but as You will."*
> *—verses 36-39 (NIV)*

I believe that Jesus, in this crisis of His life, was led by the Holy Spirit to pray.

THE HOLY SPIRIT WILL ADD SPECIAL DEPTH, POWER, AND FAITH TO OUR PRAYER

The Holy Spirit will not only direct us to pray for those special needs, but He will join us in our praying with a depth of power and faith that we do not have by ourselves. We are weak in and of ourselves, and therefore, our prayers are weak, but when the Holy Spirit fills us, He will pick up where our weakness ends, and His praying will transcend any possible praying on our part. You see, He calls us to prayer, He shows us our needs, but then He joins us in prayer as our loving prayer partner, adding infinite understanding, desire, and power to the prayers we are making.

> **THE HOLY SPIRIT WILL NOT ONLY DIRECT US TO PRAY FOR THOSE SPECIAL NEEDS, BUT HE WILL JOIN US IN OUR PRAYING WITH A DEPTH OF POWER AND FAITH THAT WE DO NOT HAVE BY OURSELVES.**

Paul puts it like this in Romans 8:26 (NKJV): "The Spirit Himself makes intercession for us with groanings which cannot be uttered." Our intercessor, the Holy Spirit, prays with such fervency that it is groans that cannot be put into words. Oh, what an encouragement when we go to prayer! If the Holy Spirit is filling us, and we are walking by the Spirit, and being led by the Spirit, we have a prayer partner who will help us pray. Let me encourage you to allow the Holy Spirit to pray through you in tongues and intercede for you. The Holy Spirit knows your heart and everything that concerns you and knows more than anyone exactly what you need at every moment. The more you allow Him to pray through you in tongues, the more you will experience the will of God.

As you allow the Holy Spirit to pray through you, you will experience the refreshing or drenching of the Holy Spirit. If you allow the Holy Spirit to pray through you daily you will experience a daily renewal and refreshing. As you pray in the Holy Spirit, your relationship with your heavenly Father will grow stronger and stronger. This relationship will become the greatest adventure as you discover that the Holy Spirit is leading the way for you to fulfill the destiny God designed for you before He placed you in your mother's womb.

Pray with me:

Dear heavenly Father, I humble myself before You and yield myself to the Holy Spirit living in me. Holy Spirit, I give myself to You and allow Your spiritual languages to flow out of my being so that You may pray to my heavenly Father in Your perfect will and way. In Jesus's name. Amen.

CHAPTER 7

YOUR HOLY TOUR GUIDE

LED BY THE SPIRIT

A s I have enjoyed this drenching relationship with our heavenly Father, through the person of the Holy Spirit, an incredible opportunity was made available to me and my wife, Joy. We had the opportunity to visit the Holy Land—Israel—the land of the Bible, and the place I had read so much about. We were invited to go with a group of other people and tour. It was our first trip to this area, and I was extremely excited. I began reading and rereading the Bible, looking forward to seeing so much of what I was reading and imagining what the tour was going to be like. After we arrived, checked in at our hotel, and got settled into our room, we all gathered to meet with our official tour guide.

Our guide had been leading tours for many years, and he was extremely knowledgeable of the Bible and the history of Israel. It was fascinating to hear him narrate our tour day after day. Every evening, when we would return to our room, I would search the Bible and review all the places we had been and all the sites we had seen. Every day with our tour guide was overflowing with revelation about this land and the Bible. The tour guide opened my eyes to so many things that the Bible was literally coming alive to me in a way I had never experienced. Every day was exciting and filled with wonder, discovery, and adventure. I didn't want to leave; I wanted to stay with the tour guide and continue to experience the wonderful journey he had taken us on. We are still living with the burning desire to return to the Holy Land and tour again.

Many times, I have reminisced about that trip and how valuable the tour guide was. If we had not had the tour guide to lead the way, we would have missed out on so much that made the adventure so powerful and exciting. We could have also put ourselves in some potentially dangerous situations. There is no doubt we definitely needed that guide. The guide had already been there over and over and knew what was ahead of us, what to avoid, and which direction we needed to go.

We are all on a journey, and we need the best tour guide. When we try to take the journey without a guide, we are easily confused, misdirected, and, sometimes, even lost along the way. However, with a good guide at your side, you can rest assured that you will not get hurt or lost as you explore, and you'll conclude your experience with a wonderful memory of a trip well-executed.

JUST AS A GUIDE LEADS A GROUP THROUGH A HISTORICAL SITE, THE HOLY SPIRIT WANTS TO GUIDE US THROUGH LIFE.

With this example in mind, let's look at John 16:13 (KJV), where Jesus told His disciples, "Howbeit, when he, the Spirit of truth is come, he will guide you into all truth." In this verse, Jesus used the example of a tour guide to describe the guiding ministry of the Holy Spirit. Just as a guide leads a group through a historical site, the Holy Spirit wants to guide us through life.

As we have seen, a tour guide is a professional who has gained intimate knowledge, through years of dedication and experience, of a site you want to see. He knows all the shortcuts and all the points of interest, and he can relate its history in depth. Your willingness to allow the guide to lead and your willingness to follow his directions will save you from making mistakes and drawing incorrect conclusions about where you are, where you are headed, and what you are seeing.

Jesus was informing us that if we are willing to listen to the Holy Spirit and follow His instructions, He will act as a guide. Like the tour guide I shared with you earlier, the Holy Spirit knows what lies ahead of us. He knows the obstacles we should avoid; He sees our ultimate destination, and He knows God's plan for us down to the smallest detail. The Holy Spirit knows every route God desires for us to take, and if we are willing to follow the Spirit's leading, He will give us a wonderful and memorable experience along the journey.

I want to tell you that the Holy Spirit deeply desires to guide you on your journey. If you'll let Him, He will offer you sound guidance in every sphere of life. If you listen to His voice, He will help you with decisions you need to make about your career, marriage, where you should live, etc. He is the only One who knows the future; therefore, He is the only One who is truly qualified to lead and guide you.

Divine guidance is one of the biggest challenges we face in the Christian life. However, Jesus explicitly said that the Holy Spirit is here to lead us every step along the way. What a relief and security it affords us to know that God the Father has charged the Holy Spirit with the responsibility of leading and guiding us to the right place at the right time—every single time. He also warns us *away from* certain people, places, and situations. This is His job! Without His direction, we are incapable of discerning where we should go, the people with whom we should surround ourselves, and the best timing for our endeavors.

However, in order for this to happen, we have to make an effort to listen to the Holy Spirit's voice and be willing to follow His instruction. If we will do that, we'll find that the Spirit of God is leading us, just as He did the apostles in the book of Acts!

Today, I urge you to open your heart to the guiding ministry of the Holy Spirit. Trust that He is the Spirit of truth who will not mislead you. Take the hand of the Holy Spirit and tell Him from your heart: *Holy Spirit, I trust You from this moment forward to be my guide every step of the way!*

Our entire lives are made up of the decisions we have made and the ones we are going to make. How many times have we all made poor decisions? How many times have we wished we could go back and undo some of those decisions? Every decision will bring success, disappointment, or regret into our lives. Every decision has consequences, and the potential for error is great because we are all imperfect human beings. Many times, we are living under the pressure and stress that come with making decisions.

Sometimes, we torture ourselves with questions. *What am I going to do? Which way am I going to go? Who is going to help me? How is it going to work out?* What is the answer?

THE BIBLE TEACHES US THAT LIFE IS A JOURNEY, AND GOD HAS GIVEN US A ROADMAP FOR LIFE. THE BIBLE IS OUR ROADMAP.

The answer is to let the Holy Spirit be your guide. Let the Holy Spirit lead the way for you. The Bible teaches us that life is a journey, and God has given us a roadmap for life. The Bible is our roadmap, and that is why it is so important that we read it and reread it, memorize, meditate on, and obey what it says, and make all our decisions based on what it says. God has given us a compass, and that's our conscience that keeps us moving in the right direction if we will listen to it. God has even given us a personal guidance counselor, the Holy Spirit.

The Bible is clear that God wants to lead us along the right paths. God doesn't want us to make poor choices and mess up. The Bible says that God wants to lead us in paths of righteousness for His name's sake (see Psalm 23). That means God wants to keep us on the right track. God has good plans already laid out for you, not bad plans. Our God is good, and He has promised to give us His guidance. God is not trying to keep His plans and guidance for you a secret. God wants you to know how to follow His guidance.

First and foremost, God must be number one. God must be in first place. You have to decide what is going to be first in your life. If the Holy Spirit is going to be your guide, then you must make up your mind that God is going to be first, above everyone and all things.

You cannot follow a world that does not follow God. You cannot serve God and money, you cannot serve God and anything else, you have got to make up your mind about who or what is going to be number one in your life. There can only be one number one. You cannot conform to this world and be just like everybody else and be led by the Holy Spirit because He's going in a different direction. Romans 12:2 (author paraphrase) says, "Do not be conformed to this world (do not copy the behavior or values of this world) but be transformed (let God transform you)." The major reason so many do not know what God wants them to do is because they are deeply rooted in this world's system and ways of doing things, you cannot think like the world and think like God thinks. God's plans for you are good. God wants you to overflow with His joy and peace, but those things are not found in this world.

If you want to be led by the Holy Spirit, you cannot follow friends that are not being led by God. You have to stop allowing friends to influence your direction. One of the major reasons people miss God's will for their lives, God's perfect, good, and pleasing plan for their life is because of peer pressure. Proverbs 13:20 says we should keep company with wise friends, and we'll become wise. But if we associate with fools, our lives will suffer great hurt. Make sure your advice is coming from the right source. God wants you to have friends who are unbelievers, but you are to influence them; do not let them influence you. We are to love the people, no matter what kind of lifestyle they live, but we are to hate the world's system of prejudices, racism, injustice, and sexism, and people hurting each other, envy, strife, division, etc. Love the people, hate the world's system.

To be led by the Holy Spirit, there are some things we must stop doing. Stop following a world that does not follow God. Stop following friends who are not led by God. Stop allowing other things to be your source and make God your number one source. Stop allowing your circumstances and emotions to lead you.

To be led by the Holy Spirit, there are some things we must start doing. We must have a determined desire to be led by God. We must be willing and obedient to God. We must be willing to obey God in advance before we even know what God wants us to do. We must always line ourselves up with what the Bible says. God wants us to obey what we already know before He reveals to us something new. God never contradicts His Word. The more you read the Bible, the more God will guide you.

TO BE LED BY THE HOLY SPIRIT, WE MUST ALWAYS ASK HIM TO LEAD US.

To be led by the Holy Spirit, we must always ask Him to lead us. Psalm 25:9 (NIV) says, "He guides the humble in what is right and teaches them His way." To be led by the Holy Spirit, we must train ourselves to listen carefully to His voice. When we are praying and reading God's Word, we must take the time to wait patiently in His presence, sit quietly before Him, and give Him some of our very best quality private time.

Back to my experience with the tour guide that led the way on our trip to Israel. Every morning, we had to connect with our tour guide. Let me encourage you to reconnect with your tour guide (the Holy Spirit) every morning.

All throughout the day and every step of the way, we had to stay connected to our tour guide. It could have been very dangerous to get distracted and wander away from our guide. On our journey through this temporary world, we can easily be distracted and tempted to follow our own desires and find ourselves confused, in dangerous situations, etc. It is very important for us to stay connected to the Holy Spirit every step of the way all through the day, as He is leading us in a safe and secure direction.

As we stayed connected, our relationship with the tour guide grew closer, stronger, and more trusting. As you stay connected to the Holy Spirit, your relationship with Him will grow closer, stronger, and more trusting.

All along the way, there were some sites that were blocked off from the general public, and there were armed guards to keep everyone out, however, our tour guide had exceptional access and went ahead of us and cleared our entrance with the guards, and the guards removed the blockages so we could gain access. The Holy Spirit is always with you to go before you and address any obstacle or blockage that may hinder you from gaining access to the opportunities God has for you to experience on your journey.

On one occasion, our tour bus stopped, and an intruder tried to gain access to our bus. The intruder was a peddler wanting to sell us his merchandise. However, the tour guide stood in the doorway of our bus and explained to us the intruder's intentions and then refused to give him access. In the same way, the Holy Spirit is always standing at the entrances of our lives to warn us of intruders and their intentions; the Holy Spirit is always making a way for us to avoid those temptations.

The Holy Spirit is always guiding us. He intends for us to be in the right places, at the right times, doing the right things, with the right people so that God will be honored and glorified through us so that we can successfully accomplish all the plans God has for us.

Pray this prayer with me, Holy Spirit, I open my heart to Your leadership and guidance in my life. I repent for foolishly having tried to lead myself through difficult decisions and questions, when you were always right there, wanting to lead me along the way. You know the plan of God for me down to the smallest detail, and from this time forward, I will do my best to consult You and to yield to Your guidance for my life. You know everything about me, my future, and which steps I need to take next. Rather than try to figure it all out on my own, I entrust myself to you as my official Guide to lead me each step of the way!

CHAPTER 8

YOU ARE NEVER ALONE

WALKING IN THE SPIRIT

I am about to write some words you need to get deep into your spirit and consistently remind yourself of. Are you ready? Underline these words, "You Are Never Alone!" Highlight these words, "You Are Never Alone!" Remind yourself over and over again and again, "You Are Never Alone!" The Holy Spirit is living on the inside of you. The Holy Spirit is always with you. Everywhere you go, and every moment of every day and every night, the Holy Spirit is always with you. He is always waiting for you to acknowledge that He is with you. He is always waiting for you to ask Him for His help and assistance in every area and situation. He is the highest intelligence in the universe. He is the Spirit of all knowledge and wisdom. If you will follow His direction and obey His instructions, you will experience His strength, peace, and rest. As you learn to be submissive to Him in every way, you will find yourself walking in the Spirit.

Your heavenly Father sent the Holy Spirit to you at the request of your Savior Jesus Christ so that you could walk in the Spirit every day. The Holy Spirit lives in your body. Your human body is the temple of the Holy Spirit. The Holy Spirit wants to see through your eyes. He wants to hear through your ears. He wants to speak through your mouth. He wants to work through your hands. He wants to walk in your feet. He wants His thoughts to flow through your mind. He wants to burn in your heart, and He wants your human spirit to be in unity and partnership with Him continually. He wants your eyes to see things as He sees them. He wants your ears to hear His voice. He also wants you to hear things the way He hears them. He wants you to receive the things that He has planned and prepared for you.

EVERYWHERE YOU GO, AND EVERY MOMENT OF EVERY DAY AND EVERY NIGHT, THE HOLY SPIRIT IS ALWAYS WITH YOU.

I have been in this drenching relationship with the Holy Spirit for forty-three years at the time of this writing. It has been beyond amazing in every sense of the word. It has been and continues to be a daily adventure of discovery. The Holy Spirit is the best friend you will ever have. On the first Sunday of January 2021, I tested positive for the coronavirus or COVID-19. On the second Sunday of January 2021, I was in the hospital intensive care unit struggling for my life. The virus had been running rampant around the globe at that time for approximately a year or so. I had heard the reports of all the people sick and dying from the virus. I had also heard the main treatment for those in hospitals was to put them on ventilators.

A few months before I was infected with the virus, something inside of me (I believe with all my heart it was the Holy Spirit) directed me that if I got the virus, I would not allow them to put me on a ventilator. I told my wife that if I got the virus, she was not to allow them to put me on a ventilator. After I had been in the hospital intensive care unit for approximately twenty minutes, a doctor came in, looked at me, and said, "We need to go ahead and get you on a ventilator."

I said to the doctor, "Oh, no, we are not going to do that. We are going to do everything we can without a ventilator."

I was in the hospital intensive care unit for thirty-two days, and many times, the doctors and nurses told my wife they didn't think I was going to survive and tried to convince her to permit them to put me on a ventilator. I'm so very thankful my wife supported my faith in God and my decision to stay off the ventilator. I give all the credit to God the Holy Spirit for directing me to stay off it. Many amazing and miraculous things happened while I was fighting off the attack on my body. But during the attack, I rediscovered things that I already knew about the Holy Spirit, and I also discovered some incredible things about the Holy Spirit that gave me fresh strength and fresh life while I was going through the battle.

There are so many amazing things I could share right here. But I want to share with you one of the reasons this drenching is so necessary and important when it comes to understanding what it means to walk in the Spirit. To walk in the Spirit means you are not walking alone! The hospital would not allow me to have any visitors; I was alone, fighting for my life. This is another reason why this drenching is so important. The Holy Spirit inside you is your friend and your partner. He is much stronger than you, and He is always encouraging you, supporting you, and fighting for those who will walk with Him.

While I was in the hospital fighting for my life, my body began to deteriorate. I weighed 196 pounds before the virus, but my body began to lose weight rapidly, and I lost over 50 pounds. My muscles atrophied. I did not have the strength to even turn my body over in the bed. My mind was disconnected from my routine way of thinking; my mind was extremely focused on breathing, fighting to keep my oxygen level as high as I possibly could. I'm not sure what to call what I am about to share with you. But, it happened multiple times before I realized what was happening to me. I would wake up from sleep (at least, I think I was waking up from sleep), and I could see my body lying on the bed. I could see and hear all the machines hooked up to me. Everything seemed normal until a nurse or a doctor would come into the room, and then instantly, I would be looking up from the bed at them.

This experience happened several times before I began to realize that my spirit was out of my body and on the other side of the room. As these experiences continued to happen, I began to not only realize my spirit was out of my body, but I also began to realize that while my spirit was on the other side of the room, it was not alone. There was another Spirit with me. I realized that the Holy Spirit was with me, He was a very strong Spirit, and He was holding onto me. This is when my faith leaped, and I knew I was not going to die. I began to realize that my spirit

YOU ARE NEVER ALONE   121

was stronger than my body and my mind. I already knew that we are three-part beings. We are spirits, we have souls (minds, wills, and emotions), and we live in bodies (flesh, blood, and bones). I also realized that no matter what was going on with my body or with my mind, I was not alone. The Holy Spirit was with me and more real than I had ever experienced. I began to talk to the Holy Spirit with courage and confidence; I had no fear, worry, or doubt that my friend was there for me, and all He needed me to do was trust Him and keep on walking in the Spirit with Him.

My health did not return instantly, but I began to improve. I came home from the hospital and have returned to my family and the ministry God has given me. Now, I am sharing this drenching relationship with you. God does not love me more than He loves you or anyone else. He wants you to walk in the Spirit with Him every day.

In the Bible, the apostle Paul writes about walking in the Spirit:

This I say then, Walk in the Spirit, and ye shall not fulfill the lust of the flesh. For the flesh lusteth against the Spirit, and the Spirit against the flesh: and these are contrary the one to the other: so that ye cannot do the things that ye would. But if ye be led of the Spirit, ye are not under the law. Now the works of the flesh are manifest, which are these; Adultery, fornication, uncleanness, lasciviousness, Idolatry, witchcraft, hatred, variance, emulations, wrath, strife, seditions, heresies, Envyings, murders, drunkenness, revellings, and such like: of the which I tell you before, as I have also told you in time past, that they which do such things shall not inherit the kingdom of God. But the fruit of the Spirit is love, joy, peace, longsuffering, gentleness, goodness, faith, Meekness, temperance: against such there is no law. And they that are Christ's have crucified the flesh with the affections and lusts. If we live in the Spirit, let us also walk in the Spirit. Let us not be desirous of vain glory, provoking one another, envying one another. —Galatians 5:16-26 (KJV)

EVERY DAY, YOU ARE EITHER WALKING IN YOUR FLESH OR YOU ARE WALKING IN THE SPIRIT. WE MUST BE AWARE OF THIS AND CHOOSE TO OVERRIDE OUR FLESH AND BE DETERMINED TO WALK IN THE SPIRIT.

Every day, you are either walking in your flesh or you are walking in the Spirit. We must be aware of this and choose to override our flesh and be determined to walk in the Spirit. The Holy Spirit knows everything. The Holy Spirit is everywhere all at the same time. The Holy Spirit is all-powerful and stronger than all our adversaries, including our flesh. Every day, all through the day, remind yourself, to choose to deny your flesh and bring your flesh with all its desires and temptations into submission to the Holy Spirit living in you! You are not alone; the Holy Spirit is living in you. He will not override your will, desires, or emotions, but if you choose to ask Him for His help and then follow His direction and obey His instructions, you can walk in His Spirit and be successful and victorious. The Holy Spirit enables us to do things we would never be able to do on our own.

You can walk in the Spirit 24/7. You aren't meant to let your flesh rule—you're meant to walk in the spirit and live on a higher level, where victory reigns and righteousness rules. The flesh is loud and demanding. Your flesh will scream at you and try to demand you to give in to its desires. It likes to have its way, and it sure doesn't give up easily. It may not seem like it, but you have control over what controls *you*. Make up your mind not to allow your flesh to control you.

You can walk in the Spirit if you want to, but it's a choice you must make continually. The Holy Spirit is living on the inside of you right now. He is in you right now; He is speaking and offering you His direction and instructions. God has big plans for you, and He has placed everything you need to live and succeed on the inside of you. His Spirit living inside of you is ready to help you walk it out. Walking in the Spirit is how God makes your dreams and desires come to pass.

IT IS NOT GOD'S PLAN FOR YOU TO LIVE DISCOURAGED AND DEFEATED. THE BETTER LIFE IS WAITING FOR YOU TO OVERRIDE YOUR FLESH AND WALK IN THE SPIRIT.

It is not God's plan for you to live discouraged and defeated. The better life is waiting for you to override your flesh and walk in the Spirit. This kind of life doesn't happen instantly or overnight. This is a lifestyle and a lifelong growing and learning relationship with God. When you choose to walk in the Spirit, with every act of obedience to God, you get closer to God, and your life is transformed more and more like Him.

There are some things you can do to help you walk in the Spirit. When you walk in the Spirit, you become more aware of God's presence and how He'll never leave you alone. The more we walk in the Spirit, the less lonely we feel in any and every circumstance because we are more attuned to His presence.

GET RID OF EVERYTHING THAT HINDERS

Hebrews 12:1 (NIV) states, "Therefore, since we are surrounded by such a great cloud of witnesses, let us throw off everything that hinders and the sin that so easily entangles. And let us run with perseverance the race marked out for us." Examine yourself, then. Give your life a thorough inspection. Look for anything that hinders you from being pleasing to God or closer to God. Especially get rid of any sins that are easy for you to give in to.

The Bible doesn't teach us to gradually slow down, wean ourselves off, stop just a little at a time, and eventually remove hindrances and sins. The Bible uses terms like lay aside, get rid of, or throw off. This means we must aggressively remove the hindrances and sins from our lives. If you fell into a bee hive or a hornet's nest, you would not gently and gradually remove the painful pests from your body. Without any hesitation and with aggressive action, you would separate yourself from them because you know how dangerous, painful, and potentially deadly it is for you to remain in that condition.

This is not something you need to compromise with or waste time wondering if it's a good idea. The hindrances and sins that we allow to remain give Satan legal territory in our lives to entangle and enslave us. We must aggressively drive the devil out. We drive him out by getting rid of all sins; this slams the doors in the devil's face. When we repent for allowing hindrances and committing sins, it takes away Satan's legal access to our lives. The Bible clearly says to give no place to the devil.

Anything that does not line up with the Word of God is a hindrance, and we must address and remove it. Satan wants to strap hindrances onto us like heavy weights to slow us down and keep us from the incredible promises and blessings God has for us to receive and enjoy. Hindrances are anger, rage, envy, striving, unforgiveness, cursing, slander, lying, false accusations, gossip, foul, abusive, shameful language, joking and conversations, unclean and unholy desires, sexual impurity and perversion, adultery, fornication, idolatry, witchcraft, hatred, strife, envy, murders, drunkenness and anything like them (see Colossians 3:5-6 and Galatians 5:19).

We do this by doing what Hebrews 12:2 (NIV) says: "fixing our eyes on Jesus." To get rid of those things that are slowing you down, and to walk in the spirit, the natural world has to become small in your heart and mind, while the things of God become bigger and bigger. If you have a sinful habit—something you know isn't pleasing to God—now is the time to rid yourself of it as fast as you would get away from a hornet's nest.

Maybe there are some things you watch on television you shouldn't be watching. Things that drain your spirit. There are times when you need to say no out loud when something is displeasing to the Father. Even shout it out if you need to. Say, "No, I do not receive that. I cast down every high imagination that tries to exalt itself against God."

Allow the Holy Spirit to correct and guide you as you work toward walking in the Spirit every day. He will help you not only to separate yourself from the world but to desire the things of God more than anything else.

ALLOW THE HOLY SPIRIT TO CORRECT AND GUIDE YOU AS YOU WORK TOWARD WALKING IN THE SPIRIT EVERY DAY.

YOU WILL REAP WHAT YOU SOW

Galatians 6:7-8 (NLT) says,

> *Don't be misled—you cannot mock the justice of God. You will always harvest what you plant. Those who live only to satisfy their sinful nature will harvest decay and death from that sinful nature. But those who live to please the Spirit will harvest everlasting life from the Spirit.*

One of the very best ways to walk in the Spirit is by sowing and reaping. And one of the best things you can sow to reap an amazing harvest is your TIME. Many people cannot walk in the

Spirit because they do not take the time to feed themselves the Word of God. If you do not give God some of your time, other voices will plant seeds in your life and choke the Word of God out.

We all have things we have to do in the natural, but those things must not be allowed to take up ALL of our time. We must allow our spirit to feed on God's Word, to fellowship with the Holy Spirit, and build our faith by praying in the Holy Spirit (Jude 20). The truth is the devil doesn't want you to have time. He will do anything and everything he can to take away your time. If you are going to sow time, you will have to MAKE TIME. Be determined to make some time for God every day.

When you sow to the spirit, it will take you into a realm where you've never been before. When you get to a place where the truth of God's Word is so real, the Spirit of God will rise on the inside of you, and you'll do things you never would have done before.

GIVE YOUR BODY TO GOD

Romans 12:1-2 (NLT) describes the drenched life like this:

> *And so, dear brothers and sisters, I plead with you to give your bodies to God because of all he has done for you. Let them be a living and holy sacrifice—the kind he will find acceptable. This is truly the way to worship him. Don't copy the behavior and customs of this world, but let God transform you into a new person by changing the way you think. Then you will learn to know God's will for you, which is good and pleasing and perfect.*

Now, that may sound like a big commitment. And it is! But that's what Jesus did for us! He presented His body as a living sacrifice on the cross. We must also crucify our bodies daily, not in a physically abusive manner, but by bringing our bodies into submission to God's Word and the Holy Spirit that lives in our bodies.

We do this by laying aside the things of the world. This means we must be willing and determined to give up activities, friends, or habits that don't line up with God's best for us. We must walk away from anything that is not pleasing to the Lord.

We do this by obeying God's Word and not our flesh. The reason sins come so easy for us, and we are so good at sinning is because we have had so much practice at sinning. Think about this: a person doesn't become an alcoholic the first time they take a drink. They take another drink and another. They keep on practicing until their flesh is trained to demand it. In the same way, we become good at obeying the Holy Spirit by practicing and practicing and practicing until we become good at it. We do this by making up our minds every day to dress ourselves with the Spirit in the same way we dress our physical bodies every day.

Every day, as you continue to give your body to the Lord, it may take some time for some things to straighten out and line up with God's Word, but if you are willing to be obedient, it will happen much sooner than you realize. Every day, as we obey the Holy Spirit's directions and instructions, the other things will begin to line up and straighten out. Every day that we give our bodies to the Lord, there will be alignment with heaven in the natural.

PRAY IN THE SPIRIT

Romans 8:26 (NIV) says that "the Spirit helps us in our weakness. We do not know what we ought to pray for, but the Spirit himself intercedes for us through wordless groans." One of the most powerful ways to walk in the Spirit is to start praying in the Spirit. Praying in the Spirit charges and strengthens your human spirit. Praying in the Spirit empowers you to overcome the weaknesses of your flesh with its bad habits and sinful desires. Praying in the Spirit makes it much easier for you to receive from God and to keep what you have received from God. Praying in the Spirit strengthens your ability to resist the devil. Praying in the Spirit causes your spirit to stand up when facing adversity. Praying in the Spirit reveals things to your spirit that you could never know by your own natural abilities.

IF YOU WANT TO GROW SPIRITUALLY AND YOU WANT YOUR FAITH TO GROW TO HIGHER LEVELS, DEDICATE SOME REAL TIME TO PRAYING IN THE SPIRIT EVERY DAY.

If you want to grow spiritually and you want your faith to grow to higher levels, dedicate some real time to praying in the Spirit every day. You will see God's power work in you so much that you will never want to make a decision without praying in the Spirit.

LEARN TO OBEY THE VOICE OF GOD

John 10:4 says that the good shepherd's sheep follow him because they know his voice. The Holy Spirit is living inside of you, and He is always ready to speak to you. He has an answer to every problem you are facing, whether financial, health, family, marriage, etc. Regardless of what the problem may be, the Holy Spirit living in you always has the answer. Just one word from the Lord is all it takes to completely turn everything around for you. These answers are available to you as you listen closely to the voice of the Holy Spirit living in you.

What you must do is ask yourself just how far you are willing to go in your walk with God. Some people say things like, "I will do anything for God," or "I would go to the jungles of Africa for God." But then God will ask them to do something right where they are or something that seems small and insignificant. If you do not obey God in the small things, He will not be able to ask you to do greater things. If you do not obey God in what you already know to do and especially what the Bible already says, God will not be able to ask you to do something incredible that you are unaware of. Many want to hear God's voice and way, and they want to do something special for God, but they won't forgive someone, or they won't stop watching ungodly television programs, visiting ungodly sites on the internet, etc. They won't spend time with God daily.

Hearing God's voice is vital to walking in the Spirit. Everything God tells you to do is important. So, line your life up with the Holy Spirit in all things, even when He's telling you something that seems insignificant, especially when He says something to you that you don't want to hear.

Grab ahold of this verse and pray it to your heavenly Father every day like this:

Dear heavenly Father, I thank You that I hear the voice of the Good Shepherd and a stranger's voice I will not follow.

When you obey the promptings of the Holy Spirit, you will be in the right place at the right time, doing the right thing with the right people. And you will have success and victory in everything you do.

WHEN YOU OBEY THE PROMPTINGS OF THE HOLY SPIRIT, YOU WILL BE IN THE RIGHT PLACE AT THE RIGHT TIME, DOING THE RIGHT THING WITH THE RIGHT PEOPLE. AND YOU WILL HAVE SUCCESS AND VICTORY IN EVERYTHING YOU DO.

When you practice these things, you will be walking in the Spirit, there will be no limit to what you can achieve. You will stop letting your flesh control you and begin living a Spirit-led life of peace, joy, and blessing beyond anything you've ever hoped or imagined. You will live the God kind of life right here on Earth! Remember, the more you walk in the Spirit, the less lonely you will feel. The Holy Spirit abides in you, and you are never alone.

Pray this prayer with me:

Heavenly Father, thank You for sending the Holy Spirit to me. Jesus, thank You for baptizing me in the Holy Spirit. Holy Spirit, thank You for abiding in me and never leaving me. Thank You for always being with me at all times and in every situation. Thank You for Your companionship and Your friendship and fellowship. Thank You for holding my hand all the way.

CHAPTER 9

THE WORSHIPERS

WORSHIPING IN THE SPIRIT

The Holy Spirit living in us continually calls us to worship our heavenly Father in spirit and truth. As a matter of fact, in the New Testament, in John 4, Jesus meets a woman drawing water from a well, and she questions Him about worship. Jesus replies that our heavenly Father is seeking worshipers. He calls them true worshipers—worshipers who will worship Him in spirit and in truth. One of the greatest responsibilities of every born-again, Holy Spirit-filled believer is to worship God in spirit and in truth. All throughout the Bible, God is calling and inviting us to worship Him. Psalm 95:6-7 (NIV) says, "Let us worship and bow down. Let us kneel before the Lord our maker, for he is our God. We are the people he watches over the flock under his care."

If we are not careful, we will mistake the very purpose for which God calls us to worship Him. All throughout the Bible, we read about all kinds of worship. We read about worship that is physical, financial, spiritual, soul, holy, sacrificial, joyful, etc. Some are acceptable to God, and some are not acceptable to God. We must be careful to offer God worship that He can accept. We must offer Him worship that blesses Him. The very object of our worship must always be Him.

ONE OF THE GREATEST RESPONSIBILITIES OF EVERY BORN-AGAIN, HOLY SPIRIT-FILLED BELIEVER IS TO WORSHIP GOD IN SPIRIT AND IN TRUTH.

No, where in the Bible does true worship include our personal preferences, feelings, ideas, or opinions on how God can be worshiped? We cannot say to God, I will worship You but in my own way. Once we choose the Living God as our God, we give up the right to worship in our own way. When we surrender our entire lives to Him and call Him our God, we are granting Him alone the right to prescribe how He desires to be worshiped.

Worship is never on our terms; worship is always on God's terms. When we worship on our own terms, worship becomes idolatry. When we make the God of all creation our God, we lose all our rights to how we will worship. The primary meaning of worship is the total giving of our will to the will of God. We no longer have any rights when it concerns worship. In Psalm 95 and many other scriptures throughout the Word of God, God calls us to bow down and kneel before the One who is our maker, the One whose sheep we are. He is not just calling us to some form of physical posture. It focuses on surrendering our will and our ways to Him. Meaning that we are granting supreme authority over us to God Himself. In worship and life, we are giving up our will in favor of His will.

As we respond to God's call to worship Him, the Holy Spirit living in us will begin the process of shaping our understanding and practice of worshiping God. Worship then becomes not only a privilege, but a challenge and then a necessity in our lives. Be aware and be prepared as you begin to grow in praising and worshiping God in ways that please and honor Him, you will discover new dimensions of saying to God, Your will is more important to me than my will.

Sometimes, we may relegate worship to the times when things are going well for us. It's easy to worship God when our relationships are good, all the bills are paid, we have something in the bank, and we are getting to take a vacation all along. However, God is still God when things are not going so well for us. True worship will be tested. We must learn to worship God when we are being challenged. We must learn to worship God through adversity and pain. God is seeking true worshipers. True worship is seen when we are under pressure.

I was a young and excited evangelist, traveling across the country from church to church and conducting revival services. My calendar was full of appointments, lives we were blessed and changed, and people were being saved, healed, delivered, and filled with the Holy Spirit. It was some of the best times of my life. Late one Friday evening after a revival service, I came into my house, and my phone was ringing. As I answered the phone, I realized it was a hospital calling about my younger brother, who had been in a tragic automobile accident. The lady on the phone said I needed to come right away. I asked questions, but that was all the information the hospital was willing to give me over the phone.

When I arrived at the hospital, I was told that I could not go back and see my brother. I was to take a seat in the waiting area, and they would call me when I could see him. Here I was, a mighty evangelist, traveling across the country preaching faith and miracles, but now I was overwhelmed with fear and worry. I couldn't sit down; I was pacing back and forth in the waiting room, and the Holy Spirit moved me to go to the restroom. I didn't need to wash my hands. I needed God to give me peace during the storm.

I went into the restroom and locked the door behind me. I began to pace the restroom floor. I was weeping, worried, and praying. All at once, the Holy Spirit moved me to look at myself in the mirror. I looked at myself, all worried and filled with fear, with tears dripping off my face. All at once, something began to rise within me, and the Holy Spirit in me began to move me to worship my God. I began to say words, like, "God, I praise You in the midst of all that is going on. I don't even know how to pray. I don't know if my brother is alive or dead. If he is alive, I have no idea what kind of damage has been done to him!" Then, with courage and strength, I began to say, "So, Father, I'm just going to praise You and worship You because You are still God! You are my God, regardless!"

A great peace began to overtake my mind, and the fear and worry immediately vanished. I washed my face and went back to the waiting room with great peace in my heart and mind. A nurse was in the waiting room asking for me. She told me my brother was asking for me. I was then overwhelmed with great relief and joy, knowing that He was alive. The nurse shared with me that I needed to prepare myself for what I was about to see. She said that his arms and legs were broken. He would probably lose most of his teeth. There was some damage to his chest, and he would need exploratory surgery to discover the extent of the damage.

I placed my hand on my brother's shoulder, and together, we began to pray and thank God for his life and the lives of the others involved. The nurse asked me to step back into the waiting room. Approximately thirty minutes later, the doors from the emergency room to the waiting room swung open, and there stood my younger brother on his own two feet, with his hands lifted high in the air. He never had surgery, he never lost a tooth, and he is now pastoring a church and winning souls to the kingdom of God. My worship was being tested.

In Genesis 22, we see the first place where worship is mentioned in the Bible. God told Abraham to go to Mt. Moriah to worship. God gave Abraham the order of the worship service. God was testing Abraham. God always tests those who call Him their God. God's plan for us is just like the plan He had for Abraham. God was growing Abraham's faith, and when God is testing your worship, He is growing your faith because He has greater things for your future. Your worship is what God is using to give you everything you need for all that is ahead of you.

Nowhere, did God say to Abraham, "Do you want to worship me? Just worship me in your own way." God called Abraham to worship. God called the place of worship. God called the way He wanted to be worshiped. God is calling us to worship Him, wherever and however He desires us to worship Him. Our obedience in worship determines what God will be able to do in our future. If you have to have your way, God will not be able to do very much in your future. If you are willing and obedient in worship, God will be able to do amazing and astonishing things in your life and your future.

Now watch this: Abraham heard God say, "The way I want you to worship Me is by offering your son Isaac on the altar as a sacrifice."

Abraham never had permission to say to God, "That's not the way I want to worship You. That's not the way I am. I don't feel like doing it that way. I don't like the music or the song. That's not my style. That's not where I want to worship. God, I don't like Your plan."

> **GOD IS GOD THE CREATOR. WE ARE THE CREATURES, AND THE CREATURES NEVER HAVE PERMISSION TO DICTATE TO THE CREATOR HOW THEY WILL WORSHIP HIM.**

True worship is a choice. We must choose to worship God's way or worship our way. The Holy Spirit is always there to encourage, inspire, and empower us to worship God's way. He helps us choose God's way over our way. God is God the Creator. We are the creatures, and the creatures never have permission to dictate to the Creator how they will worship Him.

One of the most beautiful things about God testing our worship is that God has left the teacher in the room with us, and the teacher is always ready to give us the correct answers for the test. I'm challenging you in the name of Jesus to override your will and choose God's will. I'm challenging you in the name of Jesus to override your way and choose God's way.

Something else so beautiful about Abraham's worship was what God was asking Abraham to sacrifice: Isaac. This was Abraham and Sarah's promise from God, and God was asking them to sacrifice him. This was Abraham and Sarah's miracle from God in their old age, and God was asking them to give him up. What I love about Abraham's relationship with God is that Abraham, without question, was ready to obey his God. That is when worship is more than a song and a feeling. True worship is not always something that feels good or something that you would naturally want to do. Sometimes, worship is pain, brokenness, despair, or sacrifice. If it doesn't cost you something, it doesn't mean all that much.

Abraham climbed up the mountain with tears dripping from his beard, knowing what God had said to him. Isaac carried the wood on his back and Abraham the fire in his hand. Abraham, in all his confusion and distress about what God was asking him to do said these words, "The lad and I will go yonder and worship" (Genesis 22:5, KJV).

You can read the whole story in Genesis 22. You will see how God showed up in the worship service. Once God saw Abraham's willingness and obedience, God spared Isaac's life and provided another sacrifice for the altar. Sometimes, when God puts His finger on something and asks us to sacrifice it, He may very well be testing to see if we love Him more than we love what He has put His finger on. Can we pass the test? Abraham passed the test; he was willing to do what God said, regardless of the cost. Abraham gave God true worship by giving over his will to the will of God.

God has created us as human beings with a need to worship. We are going to worship something or someone. The testing of God is to help you discover what or whom you worship. The test of worship is to help you determine who comes first. Many people miss the target when it comes to worshiping God. Many people assume that they know what worship should be like. Worship means to show worth, honor, to please, bless, love with all your heart, glorify, and show your undivided attention to someone. We give them the spotlight and serve them gladly and wholeheartedly.

When you are drenched—thoroughly covered and completely filled—with the presence of the Holy Spirit, He will always lead you to worship your heavenly Father. The Holy Spirit will grieve when you withhold your worship. True worship attracts our heavenly Father's attention. True worship always exalts Jesus. True worship is the atmosphere and environment where the Holy Spirit moves and performs the works of God in people's lives.

Throughout the Bible, you can see God calling us to worship, from Genesis to Revelation. In the Old Testament and the New Testament, He is calling us to worship. In the New Testament, when the Holy Spirit arrived in Jerusalem and filled the believers in the upper room, they had been together for approximately ten days, praying and worshiping God before the Holy Spirit came on them and filled them. The Holy Spirit came into an atmosphere and environment of worship.

In Acts 3, Peter and John met a crippled man at the beautiful gate of the temple and healed him. He immediately went into the temple, walking and leaping and praising God. It was an environment of worship.

In Acts 4, Peter and John were arrested and put on trial for the healing of the cripple man. After they testified with incredible boldness of the healing power of the Lord Jesus Christ, whom the accusers had crucified, they were released. They immediately gathered together with the church and their fellow believers, began to pray and worship, and the Holy Spirit filled them all, and they began to speak the Word of God with boldness.

When Stephen was being stoned to death, you can see the marks of worship all around him, as he was reported to have said, while he was being stoned to death, "Lord, do not hold this sin against them" (Acts 7:60, NIV).

When Paul and Silas were in a dungeon jail in Philippi, at midnight, they began to pray and sing. The jail began to shake, doors came open, every prisoner was set free, the jailer was saved, and his whole family was baptized. The Holy Spirit was moving in an atmosphere and environment of worship.

All through the book of Acts, you can see the marks of a worshiping atmosphere and environment.

My challenge to you is to become a true worshiper. Don't wait for a church service or a particular song or style or until you feel something and are moved emotionally. Worship for one reason and one reason only. Worship just because God is God! He's always been God, and He always will be God! Worship Him just because He's God!

~~~~~~

MY CHALLENGE TO YOU IS TO BECOME A TRUE WORSHIPER.

~~~~~~

As you worship the Father in spirit and truth, you will discover that the Holy Spirit will be active in you. Encourage others to worship with you. Be determined to glorify your heavenly Father and exalt Jesus Christ, and your worship will give the Holy Spirit the atmosphere and environment necessary to flow freely. Jesus said in John 7:37-39 that out of your belly (innermost being) the Holy Spirit would flow like rivers of living water. There is a river inside of you; let it flow!

Pray this prayer with me:

Heavenly Father, in the name of Jesus, I bow my heart and my life before You in worship. Holy Spirit, I yield my spirit to You and invite You to help me worship my heavenly Father in spirit and in truth. I give You my hands, my voice, and my heart. With all that I am, I worship. Holy Spirit, move in my life now, in any way you desire so that my heavenly Father may be glorified and blessed with my worship. In Jesus's name.

CHAPTER 10

YOUR OWN PERSONAL TRAINER

LEARNING ALL THINGS

Many of the most successful people in the professional world, have surrounded themselves with coaches, motivational teachers, and personal trainers. Athletes that compete in the Olympics start out very young with personal trainers. Those in professional sports start out with personal trainers, and they continue with personal trainers. No matter how successful they become, they always keep themselves surrounded by personal trainers to help them succeed, stay healthy and strong, and at their very best.

Gyms have personal trainers to help their members get the most benefit out of using their equipment and offer many kinds of programs designed to get their members in their best shape and keep them fit, but not everyone knows how to use all the different kinds of equipment available or the training programs that are being offered.

~~~~~~~~~~~~~~~~~~~~~~~~~~~~~

GOD ALSO HAS A FITNESS PROGRAM AND PLAN TO HELP EVERYONE WHO SERVES HIM. GOD HAS PROVIDED FOR US OUR VERY OWN PERSONAL TRAINER TO HELP US BE CONFORMED TO THE IMAGE OF JESUS CHRIST.

~~~~~~~~~~~~~~~~~~~~~~~~~~~~~

God also has a fitness program and plan to help everyone who serves Him. God has provided for us our very own personal trainer to help us be conformed to the image of Jesus Christ.

THE HOLY SPIRIT—OUR PERSONAL TRAINER

John 16:13 (NIV) says, "However, when He, the Spirit of truth, has come, He will guide you into all truth; for He will not speak on His own authority, but whatever He hears He will speak; and He will tell you things to come."

The Holy Spirit is our personal trainer to help us get into spiritual shape, stay in fit condition, become more like Christ, and be successful in all that God has planned for us. Our personal trainer is conditioning us to help us develop super strong prayer lives and be the most effective when we pray. Our personal trainer is conditioning us to help us study the word of God and to also bring back to our memory the things He has taught us in our study time. Our personal trainer is conditioning us to help us worship our heavenly Father in spirit and in truth and develop a worship that blesses our heavenly Father and defends us against the attacks of our adversary, the devil.

In Luke 4 and in Matthew 4, we read the account of when Jesus was being tempted by the devil. Notice that the Bible says that the Holy Spirit led Jesus into the wilderness, where He fasted for forty days. After the fast, Jesus was tempted by the devil. Notice the devil came to Jesus while Jesus was in a physically weakened condition due to forty days without food and water. Isn't that how the devil comes at us? He is always looking for us to become tired or hopes to find us in some kind of weakened condition. But notice the Holy Spirit was working in Jesus. Notice how Jesus responded. He remembered the Word of God, and by the power of the Holy Spirit, He was able to resist and rebuke the devil. The devil didn't immediately leave Jesus. The devil continued to tempt Him. Notice the Holy Spirit (our personal trainer) did not leave Jesus but brought to His memory another word from God, and Jesus was able to resist and rebuke again. And then, again, the devil tempted Jesus, but the Holy Spirit kept bringing to Jesus's memory every word He needed to continue resisting and rebuking until the devil left Jesus and angels came and ministered strength to Jesus and helped him recover.

The Holy Spirit—our personal trainer—is always with us. He is teaching us how to be successful, and when the pressure is on, He is there reminding us of all that He has taught us and coaching us to victory. If Jesus needed the Holy Spirit, we need the Holy Spirit. The Holy Spirit was there energizing and directing Jesus, giving Him what He needed to resist and rebuke the devil. The Holy Spirit—our personal trainer—is with us, energizing and directing us, giving us everything we need to overcome our adversaries and accomplish incredible exploits for God and His kingdom.

Jesus had an incredible teaching ministry while He was on the Earth. The Holy Spirit worked in Him and used Him to teach and train others how to live and do the works of God themselves. Our Father has sent to us the same Spirit who worked in Jesus and empowered Him to perform signs, wonders, and miracles and raised Christ from the dead. Even after Christ was raised from the dead and ascended back to heaven, He is now seated at the right hand of our heavenly Father, praying for us. His teaching and training ministry continues in the Spirit.

The Holy Spirit—Our Personal Trainer Is the Spirit of Truth

Look at these verses about the Holy Spirit:

- John 14:17 (NIV): "[He is] the Spirit of truth. The world cannot accept him because it neither sees him nor knows him. But you know him, for he lives with you and will be in you."
- John 15:26 (NIV): "But when the Helper comes, whom I shall send to you from the Father, the Spirit of truth who proceeds from the Father, He will testify of Me."

In naming the Holy Spirit the Spirit of truth, Jesus acknowledges that the Holy Spirit possesses all truth. His nature is truth. There is no error in Him. When He speaks to us, He conveys only truth. Since we do not know all things and need to learn and grow and develop, the Holy Spirit will guide us into all truth.

The Holy Spirit—Our Personal Trainer Guides Us Into All Truth

This can be seen most clearly in John 16:13 (NIV): "However, when He, the Spirit of truth, has come, He will guide you into all truth; for He will not speak on His own authority, but whatever He hears He will speak; and He will tell you things to come."

The Holy Spirit—Our Personal Trainer Teaches Us

- Luke 12:12 (NIV): "For the Holy Spirit will teach you at that time what you should say."
- John 14:26 (NIV): "But the Advocate, the Holy Spirit, whom the Father will send in my name, will teach you all things and will remind you of everything I have said to you."
- 1 Corinthians 2:13 (NIV): "These things we also speak, not in words which man's wisdom teaches but which the Holy Spirit teaches, comparing spiritual things with spiritual."
- 1 John 2:27 (NIV): "But the anointing which you have received from Him abides in you, and you do not need that anyone teach you; but as the same anointing teaches you concerning all things, and is true, and is not a lie, and just as it has taught you, you will abide in Him."

IN NAMING THE HOLY SPIRIT THE SPIRIT OF TRUTH, JESUS ACKNOWLEDGES THAT THE HOLY SPIRIT POSSESSES ALL TRUTH. HIS NATURE IS TRUTH. THERE IS NO ERROR IN HIM.

THE HOLY SPIRIT—OUR PERSONAL TRAINER REVEALS THINGS

There are some things that cannot be learned in any other way than the Holy Spirit revealing them to us.

- Luke 2:26 (NIV): "It had been revealed to him by the Holy Spirit that he would not die before he had seen the Lord's Messiah."
- Ephesians 3:5 (NIV): "[This] was not made known to people in other generations as it has now been revealed by the Spirit to God's holy apostles and prophets."

HOW DOES THE HOLY SPIRIT—OUR PERSONAL TRAINER TEACH US?

When you teach someone, you show or explain how to do something, to impart knowledge of or skill in, to help (someone) learn by giving lessons, to condition to a certain action or frame of mind. Look at these instances in the book of Acts of the Holy Spirit's guidance:

- Acts 8:29 (NIV): "The Spirit told Philip, 'Go to that chariot and stay near it.'"
- Acts 10:19 (NIV): "While Peter was still thinking about the vision, the Spirit said to him, 'Simon, three men are looking for you.'"
- Acts 11:12 (NIV): "The Spirit told me to have no hesitation about going with them."
- Acts 13:2 (NIV): "While they were worshiping the Lord and fasting, the Holy Spirit said, 'Set apart for me Barnabas and Saul for the work to which I have called them.'"
- Acts 15:28 "For it seemed good to the Holy Spirit and to us."
- Acts 16:6 (NIV): "Paul and his companions traveled throughout the region of Phrygia and Galatia, having been kept by the Holy Spirit from preaching the word in the province of Asia."

- Acts 16:7 (NIV): "When they came to the border of Mysia, they tried to enter Bithynia, but the Spirit of Jesus would not allow them to."
- Acts 20:23 (NIV): "I only know that in every city the Holy Spirit warns me that prison and hardships are facing me."
- Acts 21:11 (NIV): "The Holy Spirit says, 'In this way the Jewish leaders in Jerusalem will bind the owner of this belt and will hand him over to the Gentiles.'"

The Holy Spirit is right now on the Earth, living in every born-again believer, and God wants to pour out His Spirit on everyone who will receive Him. The world we live in needs the outpouring of God's Spirit. Our trainer—the Holy Spirit—wants to bring the kind of revival that God has in mind. However, the kind of revival God has in mind may not be the kind of revival that *we* have in mind. What we think God should be doing is most likely not what God thinks should be done.

There are some people doing incredible things in this world to help everyone they possibly can. We need a worldwide revival. The kind of revival God has in mind cannot come through the activities of nonprofits and charitable organizations—as wonderful and necessary as they are. It's going to take more than that. The kind of revival that God has in mind cannot come through behavior modification, legislated morality, the accomplishments of the scientific or medical communities, or through the development of some utopian society.

God tells us how His kind of worldwide revival will come in Zechariah 4:6: "Not by might nor by power, but by my Spirit." God is saying to us that the kind of worldwide revival He is going to bring will not be accomplished by the gifts, talents, abilities, efforts, intelligence, or wealth of a few overachieving individuals. It will not be accomplished through a select few ministers or ministries. God is saying that the kind of revival He has in mind will ONLY come by His Spirit, who is our personal trainer. To see God have the kind of revival He has in mind for this world, each of us must submit ourselves to the discipline, guidance, and instruction of the Holy Spirit—our personal trainer—and be completely obedient to Him.

When we make a decision and determination to get in our best shape physically, we partner with a trainer. Our trainer will put together a vigorous regimen designed to push us beyond our present limitations. Our trainer's ultimate goal is to help us obtain incredible results that we could never accomplish on our own. As born-again believers, the Holy Spirit is our personal trainer for life. He is not just concerned about our physical well-being, but He is concerned with every area of our life. God wants us to develop in His training, so we can imitate Jesus on the Earth and live the life Jesus died to give us—His abundant life.

The Holy Spirit's training has many amazing benefits for us. It brings us into who we really are and prevents us from giving up in times of adversity. Your training will bring honor to God and allow you to experience God's best. This training exalts the name of Jesus and elevates you to higher places. This training strengthens the areas of your life where you are weak and empowers you to overcome your flaws and recover from mistakes. You develop an amazing ability to discover and develop love for others and flow in the grace of God toward others continually.

The Holy Spirit will not use negative means to train you. For instance, He will not give you a disease to teach you something. But He will train you through His Word, along with the ordained, godly authority He has placed over you. Let me encourage you to pray fervently for God's guidance, submit to God's Word and to those He has placed in authority over you, and then be determined to obey the instructions He gives you. Because other lives depend on your obedience and training, your actions and behaviors will significantly affect how God can use you and affect all those around you that He is using you to influence for His kingdom.

THE HOLY SPIRIT'S TRAINING ... BRINGS US INTO WHO WE REALLY ARE.

I have asked several friends to give me some examples of something in their lives that the Holy Spirit had taught them. One friend said the Holy Spirit taught him: "Failure does not constitute who I am, but it is a temporary classroom from which comes a wealth of knowledge!" He came out of it on the other side with compassion, humility, and wisdom for application, ready the next time he finds himself tempted to move in that direction again. I share this with you to give you hope and encouragement.

I said to my friend, "Wow!" Oh, how many times have I had the Holy Spirit teach me and remind me of this incredible truth over and over again in my own life?

Another friend of mine said, "When a situation turns bad for me, I have learned to take the high ground, be nice, and praise God anyway."

I said, "Wow!" to that too! How many times the Holy Spirit has reminded me! And the list goes on:

- "The Holy Spirit taught me how to love my wife like Christ loved the church when I thought I already knew how."
- "The Holy Spirit taught me how to be a husband. My natural bent is not compassionate or nurturing. But the Holy Spirit is the perfect husband for her." And he went on to say that the best part is the Holy Spirit's provision isn't mass-produced. It is specific. "He has crafted me into the exact husband my wife needs based on her exact needs."
- "To love unconditionally. When to speak and when to be quiet. How to give grace when not deserved. Not to judge."
- "When you look at the heart of someone and not their sin. They may be a person that does a lot of things to hurt you, but you choose to love them anyway. The mother-in-law/daughter-in-law relationship is an example."
- "Sometimes, I want to blast someone for something they did or said, but I feel the Holy Spirit put His hand over my mouth. I probably would cause great hurt to someone if I said what I wanted to say."
- "Grace has to be given when someone does something to you or your family. *You* may want to destroy that person, but the Holy Spirit says to turn the other cheek."

These examples may all sound simple and practical to many, but the Holy Spirit is our personal trainer, and He is teaching us to be like Christ even in simple and practical ways. Godly training leads to a godly life!

Pray this prayer with me:

Heavenly Father, I thank You for the gift of the Holy Spirit. Not only does He convict me of my sin when I fall short daily, but He is my ever-present Help in times of need who also guides me into all truth. I admit that I need help to understand Your holy written Word.

Holy Spirit, will you give me a hunger to daily read the Bible? Supernaturally illuminate what I am reading and give me the ability to comprehend what I am studying—not just for head knowledge but to help me know You in a deeper way so that I give You the worship You deserve. Holy Spirit, teach me in very simple and practical ways to be more like Christ in my daily life and interactions with others as well. In Jesus's name. Amen.

CHAPTER 11

YOUR SAFE PLACE

HE IS YOUR COMFORTER

One of the most motivating and powerful reasons for living the drenched life is because of the peace and comfort the Holy Spirit provides for us through all of the many challenges we face almost every day. The stress and pressure we live in causes us to want to run away and find a safe place to get some peace for our minds and comfort for our emotions. The Holy Spirit is that safe place. His peace is our safe place. His comfort is our safe place.

~~~~~~~~~~~~~~~~~~~~~~~

THE HOLY SPIRIT IS OUR SAFE PLACE. HIS PEACE IS OUR SAFE PLACE. HIS COMFORT IS OUR SAFE PLACE.

~~~~~~~~~~~~~~~~~~~~~~~

We all know all too well the pressure of being overwhelmed by the challenges and hardships in life. We have all felt like we

155

were drowning in a flood of adversity, unable to find the strength to overcome it. Be encouraged; you are not alone. Everyone faces fiery trials and extreme adversity that seem too much for them to overcome. However, the Bible gives us inspiration, motivation, and guidance for navigating these tough times. Read this verse from the Old Testament that gives us some incredible insight into the comforting power of the Holy Spirit: "When the enemy comes in like a flood, the Spirit of the Lord will lift up a standard against him" (Isaiah 59:19, ESV).

In Isaiah 59, the people's sins have separated them from God. Israel has turned away from the Lord, and in doing so, they have created a separation from God that gives evil the opportunity to attack and attempt to destroy them. In the midst of the threats of their enemies, God does not forsake them, but He promises to step in and deliver them from their enemies and restore them, revive them, and make them strong again.

I love this verse: "When the enemy comes in like a flood, the Spirit of the Lord will lift up a standard against him." It is God's comforting assurance that He will put them in a safe place, protect His people, and give them peace by giving them His assistance when they are under attack. Just like He provided His peace and safety for the children of Israel, when we are under pressure, and our enemies are attempting to destroy us, God wants to step in and divinely intervene for us, reviving our hope and reminding us that we are His chosen ones and He has an unbreakable commitment to us.

The first part of the verse, "When the enemy comes in like a flood," implies we will be under intense stress, pressure, anxiety, or attack. We will face overwhelming adversity. That could be physical, financial, emotional, psychological, spiritual, etc. It includes anything that threatens to harm us or opposes God's will.

The second part of the verse says, ". . . the Spirit of the Lord will lift up a standard against him." This reveals to us that God is always with us, ready to make a way for us. The word standard is a military word. In the army of the Old Testament, there was a position in the army called the standard bearer. There was only one standard bearer. The standard bearer was the one who went out front, ahead of the rest of the army. The standard bearer lifted up the banner and threw the first blow or fired the first shot.

The Holy Spirit is our standard bearer. He is always out in front of us, ready to throw the first blow against our adversary. In other words, we are not in the battle alone; we have someone ahead of us, helping us face the pressure and overcome the challenges that come our way. He is ahead of us, creating a safe place for us to keep moving forward: in our marriages, families, finances, careers, ministries, etc.—every area of our lives that the enemies threaten. By continually seeking to live the drenched life, seeking to be thoroughly covered and completely filled with the presence of the Holy Spirit, we are allowing Him to keep us in safe places.

As believers in Christ, we are always on a spiritual battlefield, living in a spiritual war zone. That is one of the most important reasons for being continually drenched in the presence of the Holy Spirit. There is an ongoing battle between the forces of darkness and light, good and evil, in the invisible spiritual realm. This invisible realm of the spirit is very real and affects this natural and visible realm.

The apostle Paul teaches us in Ephesians 6:12 that "our struggle is not against flesh and blood, but against the rulers, against the authorities, against the powers of this dark world and against the spiritual forces of evil in the heavenly realms." Paul is teaching us and equipping us to be ready to face opposition in this invisible battle, stand strong in our faith, and have peace that God is fighting for us.

> **BY CONTINUALLY SEEKING TO LIVE THE DRENCHED LIFE, SEEKING TO BE THOROUGHLY COVERED AND COMPLETELY FILLED WITH THE PRESENCE OF THE HOLY SPIRIT, WE ARE ALLOWING HIM TO KEEP US IN SAFE PLACES.**

Paul goes further and admonishes us to prepare ourselves for spiritual battle. He instructs us in Ephesians 6:10-18 to "put on the full armor of God, so you can take your stand against the devil's schemes." He describes the armor we must put on.

- The belt of truth: Honesty and integrity in all aspects of life help protect us from the enemy's lies and deception.
- The breastplate of righteousness: Living a life of righteousness, or right-standing with God, shields our hearts from the enemy's attacks.

- The shoes of the gospel of peace: Being prepared to share the good news of Jesus Christ and living in peace with others provide a firm foundation in times of adversity.
- The shield of faith: Our faith in God's promises and His ability to protect and deliver us enables us to withstand the enemy's fiery darts.
- The helmet of salvation: Confidence in our salvation through Jesus Christ protects our minds from doubt and fear.
- The sword of the Spirit: The Word of God is a powerful weapon for combating the enemy's lies and deception, providing guidance and wisdom in times of trouble.

When we put on the armor of God, we are better prepared to face the flood of adversity that the enemy may attack us with. With God's armor on and with His help, we have the ability to succeed and conquer every challenge we face.

WITH GOD'S ARMOR ON AND WITH HIS HELP, WE HAVE THE ABILITY TO SUCCEED AND CONQUER EVERY CHALLENGE WE FACE.

Another powerful weapon we have to our advantage during times of the enemy's attacks and even in times of stress and difficulty is praising and worshiping our God in spirit and in truth. When we lift our hearts and our voices in praise and worship to our God, we are inviting the presence of God into our situation, and His presence brings strength, victory, and peace. Praising and worshiping God creates a safe place in the midst of all our challenges.

Psalm 22:3 says that God inhabits the praises of His people, and as we praise Him, we make a way for His power to be manifest. By focusing on God's goodness and magnifying His name, we shift our perspective from the flood of adversity to the One who is greater than any challenge we face.

God is our supreme and ultimate source of strength and help in times of struggle and pressure. Regardless of whether the battle is physical, emotional, or spiritual, we can count on the Lord to be there with His guidance and protection.

Let me encourage you to do the following:

- Be thankful to God and bless His name: When adversity comes, run to God in sincere and earnest prayer and meditate on the promises of His Word. He will create a safe place of comfort and guidance and get you safely through the storm.
- Remind yourself of God's faithfulness: Remind yourself of past victories where God has come through for you and made a way for you in other difficult situations. These memories will encourage your faith that the same God who has made a way for you before, will not forsake you now. God is going to come through for you again and again.
- Surround yourself with encouraging, Spirit-filled believers who will support you: You need to assemble together with a group of people (preferably a Spirit-filled church). Be faithful and dedicated to them. Get connected and engage with them faithfully. Receive their encouragement, prayer,

and strength during tough times. Offer your encouragement, prayers, and strength to them as well. We are all better together with other believers. The Bible declares that one believer can put one thousand devils on the run, but two believers can put ten thousand devils on the run. So, get connected to others and war for each other. There are victories for you ahead.

- With all your faith, stand your ground: No matter how fierce the battle rages, hold on to your faith in God's promises and His unfailing love for you.
- Seek to be drenched in the presence of the Holy Spirit every day. This is the life of success and victory. Let the Holy Spirit lead the way.

The Holy Spirit is our safe place. Again, every day, seek for a fresh drenching in the Holy Spirit. It will bring to you a powerful hope and peace when you face adversity. God is always there for you and ready to protect and guide you through every storm and challenge you face. So be drenched—thoroughly covered and completely filled—with the Holy Spirit. He has a safe place for you in every battle.

THE HOLY SPIRIT IS OUR SAFE PLACE. AGAIN, EVERY DAY, SEEK FOR A FRESH DRENCHING IN THE HOLY SPIRIT.

No matter how overwhelming our battles and struggles may seem, God will never leave us. He is always by our side, lifting up a standard against our enemies and providing the peace and strength we need to persevere. Hold on to your faith, and trust in the Lord's divine intervention. His love and support for you will never change. God has already made a way for you to overcome every challenge and win every battle.

Pray this prayer with me:

Dear heavenly Father, in the name of Your Son, Jesus, and through the power of the Holy Spirit, I want to live my life in the safe place You have provided for me. When life is hard, and I don't know what to do, help me remember that You are with me and that I am never alone. I cannot live without You. I cannot face tomorrow without the promise of Your presence. Today, I choose to walk and live under the protection of You, the Most High. In Jesus's name. Amen

CHAPTER 12

THE GENEALOGY OF AN OVERCOMER

YOU COME FROM A LONG LINE OF OVERCOMERS

The drenched life is the overcoming life. We all encounter struggles, battles, and adversity. We face challenges and difficult times. God is not causing the struggles or hard times we face, but it is in times of difficulty that the Holy Spirit helps us grow, develop, and become stronger. Times of adversity are opportunities for us to allow God's Word to come alive and encourage and direct us to overcome. We can't run from everything that's hard and expect God to deliver us instantly. God is taking what the enemy has meant for our harm and using it to stretch us, enlarge our capacity to do and experience greater things, and enable us to become the overcomer He has destined for us to be.

We must remain faithful in our relationship with the Holy Spirit during our times of adversity. We must make up our minds to serve God no matter what comes against us, and God will honor us. We must fight the good fight of faith. We must remember that God does not waste anything we go through in life. We are growing, maturing, and being prepared for higher levels of victory. We must remain faithful and continue to live the drenched life.

GOD IS TAKING WHAT THE ENEMY HAS MEANT FOR OUR HARM AND USING IT TO STRETCH US, ENLARGE OUR CAPACITY TO DO AND EXPERIENCE GREATER THINGS, AND ENABLE US TO BECOME THE OVERCOMER HE HAS DESTINED FOR US TO BE.

This life is full of battles, so we must be like soldiers in an army, ready to fight for victory! We must be mighty overcomers! We must be ready to fight because there are some things worth fighting for!

- Our marriages
- Our families
- The salvation of our loved ones and friends
- The health of our bodies
- Our finances
- The Word of God

Threats to our faith are always with us, and, as Christians, our fight is against the powers of this world that are trying to pull us away from God. God wants to train us to be mighty overcomers that conquer every challenge life brings to us! The good news is that God is ready to give us every weapon we need to win every battle we face. When we put on the armor of God's Word and remember that Jesus goes with us, we can face down every enemy and rest assured that we will come out victorious. I want to give you some verses from the Bible to help you become a strong and mighty overcomer for Christ! Mark these verses in your Bibles, read them again and again, memorize them, meditate on them, and become what these verses talk about! God wants you to be a mighty overcomer! God wants you to live in victory!

> *2 Samuel 10:12 (NKJV): "Be of good courage, and let us be strong for our people and for the cities of our God. And may the Lord do what is good in His sight."*

Our great God goes before us and sees the scope of every battle. Trusting God for the outcome is what makes us mighty overcomers.

> *1 John 5:4 (NKJV): "For whatever is born of God overcomes the world. And this is the victory that has overcome the world—our faith."*

This verse means that everyone who loves Jesus and trusts Him for their salvation is already victorious. Throughout every struggle in life, we can be calmed knowing that the outcome has already been determined, and we are on the winning side.

> *Psalm 18:39 (NKJV): "For You have armed me with strength for the battle; You have subdued under me those who rose up against me."*

There is no fear or worry that God doesn't understand. Our God sees the wars that rage within us, and He has an endless supply of strength for all of us who will turn to him. Through His Word, we can learn how to face those who oppose us without fear, rising above anything or anyone that we are threatened by.

> *Deuteronomy 20:1 (NKJV): "When you go out to battle against your enemies, and see horses and chariots and people more numerous than you, do not be afraid of them; for the Lord your God is with you, who brought you up from the land of Egypt."*

When we are overwhelmed by the fight in front of us, we can take heart that God is with us. Our heavenly Father would never leave his children to fight alone, and He is stronger than any army.

> *Psalm 44:5 (NKJV): "Through You we will push down our enemies; Through Your name we will trample those who rise up against us."*

God is reminding us that we cannot win by doing things the world's way or our own way. The battles are won by those who hold on to God and push back against the enemies until those enemies are too weak to stand any longer. This kind of victory comes through trusting God in every step and standing strong even when you may seem to be losing ground.

> *Psalm 28:7 (NKJV): "The Lord is my strength and my shield; My heart trusted in Him, and I am helped; Therefore my heart greatly rejoices, And with my song I will praise Him."*

Jesus is the ultimate overcomer and our greatest protector. When we hold up our troubles against His truth, we are shielded from the worry and fear that so often come to rob us of our faith and defeat us. Our loudest battle cry should always be one of praise to Christ for His protection because the Bible tells us that God will never give us more than we can handle.

2 Corinthians 4:7-9 (NKJV): "But we have this treasure in earthen vessels, that the excellence of the power may be of God and not of us. We are hard-pressed on every side, yet not crushed; we are perplexed, but not in despair; persecuted, but not forsaken; struck down, but not destroyed."

Many times, during the heat of the battle, we feel like the battle is too hot, and we are going to be defeated, but God is with us in the heat of the battle and will never let us be defeated. Sometimes, during the battle, we get tired and weary, but we have God's promise that if we keep on fighting, we will have the victory. When we grow weary, what is important to remember is that God knows how much we can take better than we know ourselves, and He is not going to allow us to be defeated. He is not letting us down or leaving us; He is growing us in our strength.

WE ARE HIS MIGHTY OVERCOMERS, AND HE IS MAKING US STRONGER AND STRONGER!

We are His mighty overcomers, and He is making us stronger and stronger! Today, you are stronger than you have ever been! If we are going to be mighty overcomers in God's army, we have to stand strong in the heat of battles and allow God to develop His strength within us. We may fall, but we will never stay down, like it says in Proverbs 24:16 (NIV): "Though the righteous fall seven times, they rise again." Through life's battles, God has shown us that when we fight with Him, we cannot be defeated.

As a born-again, Spirit-filled believer, let me share with you just a little about your genealogy, where you come from, what you have in you, and what you are made out of. You are not in this battle alone, and you are not the first one to face adversity. There is a long line of others who have come before you, faced severe and extreme challenges, and overcome. God shares with us a little about some of them to encourage and inspire us to keep up the fight and press on to more great victories.

We can find many of these overcomers and their stories in the Bible. We will not only be encouraged, but we will learn from them as well. There is nothing we will face in this life that we cannot overcome! You are well able to overcome every obstacle that you will ever face.

We can read about Joseph in Genesis 37-50. Joseph stayed faithful to God and maintained his integrity through severe mis-treatment, great injustice, and tremendous hardship. Joseph's life was filled with trouble. His own brothers sold him into Egyptian slavery, where he faced adversity after adversity. He was falsely accused, thrown into prison, and forgotten about for years. Finally, after many years, he was set free from prison and became the second-in-command to the Pharaoh. Through all of Joseph's hardship and adversity, he never wavered in his commitment to God, and he was able to see how the Lord had preserved him through it all and even used it to prepare him for his destiny—that of an overcomer!

We can read about Moses in Exodus 3-4. Moses is an over-comer I can relate to. Has God ever asked you to do something that you did not believe you had the ability to do? When God met Moses at the burning bush on the back side of the desert and told him to demand that Pharaoh let God's people go, Moses explained to God why he could not do what God was telling him to do. Have you ever been there? All the way, though, God was with Moses, and God is with you and me—all the way.

We can read about Gideon in Judges 6-7. I love Gideon. He is an amazing example of an overcomer. God wanted Gideon to defeat the Midianites, but Gideon thought he was inadequate for the job; however, God gave Gideon the victory.

We can read about Samson in Judges 13-16. Regardless of how many mistakes Samson made, God heard Samson's prayers and, ultimately, gave him victory over his enemies. We can even be overcomers in death.

We can read the story of Ruth in the book of Ruth. Ruth is an example of someone who did the right thing, regardless of the perceived outcome. Doing the right thing may not be easy or yield instant results, but God sees you, and He will reward your faithfulness.

One of my favorite overcomers is David. We can read some of his story in 1 Samuel 16-17. He is an example for us of someone who put his complete faith and confidence in God when facing the giants that challenged him and came out victorious.

I love the overcomer Elijah. We can read some of his story in 1 Kings 19. I love his story because it reveals how human he really was. It beautifully reveals how God loves and cares for us when we are tired, exhausted, and think there is no way for us to win. It

also demonstrates for us that God is going to keep working His plan—even when we are worn out—and provide for us everything we need to overcome.

GOD IS GOING TO KEEP WORKING HIS PLAN—EVEN WHEN WE ARE WORN OUT—AND PROVIDE FOR US EVERYTHING WE NEED TO OVERCOME.

One of the most famous overcomers—Job—has an entire book dedicated to his overcoming life. Regardless of horrendous loss and suffering, Job kept his faith in God. God rewarded Job's steadfast faith and gave him back double for everything he had lost and suffered through. Job overcome even when life didn't make sense.

Daniel is another one of my favorites, with an entire book dedicated to his overcoming life. Daniel is another example of doing what is right, even in the face of death. Talk about overcoming!

How can we talk about overcomers without talking about the Overcomer of *all* overcomers: Jesus. We can read about His incredible victories in the books of Matthew, Mark, Luke, and John. He overcame sin, death, and the devil to bring salvation and deliverance to the whole world! And because Jesus overcame, He has empowered us to overcome as well.

Another amazing overcomer is Zacchaeus. You can read his story in Luke 19. His life is an example of someone who will do whatever it takes to get close to Jesus.

Look at Peter in Matthew 26. His story is an encouraging and inspiring example of someone who had made a major mistake, bounced back, overcame, and went on to become better, stronger, and greater. God is not ready to throw us away; He is always ready to make us an overcomer! Peter went on to be used by God to build the early church. We can read more about Peter's overcoming life in the book of Acts. If there was hope for Peter, there is hope for you and me, no matter what mistakes we've made. I'm talking about overcomers!

Talking about an overcomer, look at Paul. We can read his story beginning in Acts 9. Talk about someone who was misguided and full of life-taking mistakes! Don't let anyone bully you into believing that your mistakes or sins are unforgivable—look at the redeeming power of God in Paul's life. He was arresting followers of Christ and condemning them to death. Then, an amazing encounter with the crucified and risen Christ transformed and completely turned around his life. He became a preacher of the good news of Christ and gave us over half of the New Testament. All throughout his writings, he wanted all his readers to know that the transformation in his life was not anything of his own doing or efforts, but it was, above all, God's doing. Even facing his own death, he overcame and reminded us of the rewards that await him and every one of us who will believe and love their Lord and Savior, Jesus Christ.

Let me give you one more overcomer: Timothy. He was a very young man, and in Timothy's day, the young were looked down on when they tried to lead others. Not considered old enough or wise enough, Timothy faced opposition from those who thought he was not qualified to lead. However, his spiritual father and mentor in the faith—Paul—encouraged him to lead by example. This is great advice for all of us. If you have ever felt that you are too old, too weak, or not good enough to serve God or pursue a dream He put in your heart, cast those thoughts and feelings out of your heart and mind, and GO FOR IT! Don't worry about what others may think or say. Go for it, give it your very best, jump out there, and be an example for others to see the power of the Holy Spirit at work.

The Holy Spirit in you is making you an overcomer! He is actively at work in you, developing within you a tremendous faith in God and total and complete dependence on God. When you have faith in and you are totally dependent on God, you can overcome every sin, challenge, trial, and adversity that comes your way! We can persevere, we can stick with it, and we can stay the course! We can be determined to do whatever it takes! Our faith and complete dependence on God are what make overcoming possible!

WE ARE THE OVERCOMERS, YOU AND ME. WE ARE PERSEVERING, HOLDING ON TO OUR FAITH, AND COUNTING ON GOD TO GIVE US VICTORY ON TOP OF VICTORY!

The Bible talks about overcomers in the book of Revelation. Who are the overcomers in the book of Revelation? We are the overcomers, you and me. We are persevering, holding on to our faith, and counting on God to give us victory on top of victory!

Let me give you some more good news! No weapon formed against you shall prosper:

> *All your children will be taught by the Lord, and great will be their peace. In righteousness you will be established: Tyranny will be far from you; you will have nothing to fear. Terror will be far removed; it will not come near you. If anyone does attack you, it will not be my doing; whoever attacks you will surrender to you. "See, it is I who created the blacksmith who fans the coals into flame and forges a weapon fit for its work. And it is I who have created the destroyer to wreak havoc; no weapon forged against you will prevail, and you will refute every tongue that accuses you. This is the heritage of the servants of the Lord, and this is their vindication from me," declares the Lord.*
> —*Isaiah 54:13-17 (NIV)*

Read those words of encouragement in the midst of all that you may be going through! There is a real devil, and he has with him a host of real demons continually looking for ways to attack people. The Bible is clear that our adversary (Satan) is like a roaring lion going about to and fro, seeking those he can devour.

Satan likes to trespass and create chaos, confusion, conflict, and confrontation. He wants to stir up strife, arguments, disagreements, and division. He wants to provoke angry outbursts, hurtful offenses, and grudge-holding indifferences. He wants to turn us against those who love us and those who love us against us. He wants us to be upset, hurt, and offended by anyone and everyone. He is continuously shooting the tear gas of suspicion, accusation, and distrust. Satan wants to turn our lives into war zones and keep us in a constant fight mode.

He wants to stir up so much fear, panic, and unrest that we take on the mindset of a victim and believe that everyone and everything is against us, so we live our lives miserable and defeated, always making excuses and blaming others for all the unhappiness and misery we experience. Suppose we don't take on the victim mentality toward life. In that case, we take on the fight mode and turn into a fighter who's swinging wild blows at everything and everyone, constantly hurting and wounding ourselves and others, and it's always someone else's fault for the way things are. The devil wants to turn every situation into a battleground where he can plan, plot, and punish us for serving the God that has forever and eternally defeated him.

But I have come to you with good news! God has a battle plan for you to put the devil and his demons back into their place, under your feet, where they belong! I have come to encourage you: NO WEAPON FORMED AGAINST YOU SHALL PROSPER!

Now, there are some places that Satan loves to target and use as battlegrounds to keep us in the war zone. I want to expose some of those places and help us to understand why we are under the enemy's attack and how we can overcome it! Those places are *our minds, our families, our churches, and the heavenly places.*

Is there an overcomer reading this book? Lift up your voice and shout, "NO WEAPON FORMED AGAINST ME SHALL PROSPER!"

IS THERE AN OVERCOMER READING THIS BOOK? LIFT UP YOUR VOICE AND SHOUT, "NO WEAPON FORMED AGAINST ME SHALL PROSPER!"

God has given us a battle plan, and it starts right here:

Be self-controlled and alert: because your enemy, the devil, prowls around like a roaring lion looking for someone to devour. Resist him and stand firm in the faith.
—*1 Peter 5:8-9 (NIV)*

Lift up your voice and shout, "NO WEAPON FORMED AGAINST ME SHALL PROSPER!"

God has orchestrated the events in your life for you to be right where you are because He is going to empower you to overcome every attack Satan has launched against you! As children of God, we come from a long line of overcomers!

You know the story of how God spoke to Moses from the burning bush and told him to go to the Pharaoh and demand that he let the children of Israel go because God was tired of them living their lives in slavery? Well, God is also tired of the slavery and bondage that we have been living in, and He wants to break the slavery and bondage off of us as well. Keep in mind that when Moses went to Pharaoh and began to demand that he let God's children go, it angered Pharaoh, and he refused to let them go. You see, Satan is afraid and threatened that you are going to come out of the bondage you have been living in; it scares and upsets him. Lift up your voice and shout, "I'm coming out!"

Pharaoh started attacking the children of Israel. He didn't attack them because they were weak, pitiful, and worthless, because they had no future, or because they had no power. He attacked them because they were mighty and strong and growing and had potential.

I'm writing to somebody who is up under attack. That devil is not attacking you because you're a nothing and a nobody. He's attacking you because he's afraid of you. He's afraid of your power. He's afraid of your influence.

Somebody is reading this book because God wants you to understand what the battle is about and why it has come to you. Maybe you don't think you have power, influence, or potential because you're under attack, but the attack is a sign that you do have power, influence, and potential. The devil's afraid of you! The devil's afraid of you! The devil's afraid of you! That's why he's attacking your body with weakness and sickness, stealing the happiness and romance from your marriage, pilfering your money, and taking things from you that you need.

Just like Pharaoh told Moses that he was going to keep the Israelites in bondage, making bricks—but without the necessary straw to hold them together, the enemy is taking your strength, your happiness, and your opportunities to make money, advance, increase, and get ahead. The devil's plan is to put us in a position where we need more than we have access to because if he lets us have too much, he's not going be able to control us. However, you disarm the devil when you keep on making bricks anyway—when you don't have enough, but you make the ends meet anyway!

Lift up your voice and say the following:

"I had to do it anyway!"

"I was broke, but I did it anyway!"

"I was depressed, but I did it anyway!"

"I was a single parent, but I raised those kids anyway!"

"I was lonely, but I did it anyway!"

"I had to catch a ride to work, but I showed up anyway!"

"I didn't have all the things I needed, but I did it anyway!"

Lift up your voice and say, "I did it anyway!"

Check out these scriptures:

- John 16:33 (NIV): "I have told you these things, so that in me you might have peace. In this world you will have trouble. But take heart! I have overcome the world."
- Luke 10:19 (NIV): "Behold, I have given you authority to tread on serpents and scorpions and over all the power of the enemy, and nothing shall hurt you."
- Deuteronomy 28:7 (NIV): "The Lord will cause your enemies that rise against you to be defeated before you. They shall come out against you one way and flee before you seven ways."

THE ATTACK OF THE ENEMY IS YOUR CONFIRMATION THAT YOU BELONG TO THE KING OF THE UNIVERSE, AND HE HAS ANOINTED AND COMMISSIONED YOU.

The attack of the enemy is your confirmation that you belong to the King of the universe, and He has anointed and commissioned you. You are walking in His will, and you are pleasing your heavenly Father. You are a person the devil is going to forever wish he never messed with! Keep up the fight!

Remember what 2 Corinthians 10:4 (KJV) says: "For the weapons of our warfare are not carnal, but mighty through God to the pulling down of strongholds."

Fight with your prayers!

Fight with God's Word!

Fight with your worship!

Shout some praise to God right now just to let the devil know you are not out of ammunition! Let the devil know there is still a whole lot of fight left in you! And, by the way, your praise is what causes God to send reinforcements onto the battlefield, so praise and worship God in the heat of the battle, for God inhabits the praises of His people. God will come out on that battlefield to collect His praises, and He will destroy every enemy that tries to get between Him and your praises.

Take a break right here, and give God some praise right now! Praise your way to victory, for the Lord says the battle is not yours, but it's His (see 2 Chronicles 20). Let praises fill the atmosphere around you. They will penetrate the battleground and confuse the enemy. Instead of fear and anguish, begin to sing praises unto the Lord.

Truly, God would say:

- Let your voice be heard in worship of Me.
- I will inhabit your praises, and the enemy will not be able to stand the sound of your voice.

- The powers of darkness cannot tolerate My resounding voice and will not be able to withstand your praise and worship of Me.
- Give Me glory that is due My name.
- For I will do great and mighty things in the midst of you.
- I will show Myself to be strong in your midst and on your behalf.
- Watch as the enemy screams and runs in terror when I show up and bare My holy arm.
- I will be a terror to those who terrorize you.
- I AM the Almighty, and I will never be intimidated or threatened.
- I will not be silenced, and I cannot be defeated.
- Let your praise be heard, and worship Me from your heart.
- I will invade the enemy camp with a mighty force of My Spirit and enforce My kingdom as you worship, honor, and praise Me.
- Your praise will break the bondage of the enemy, loose the shackles, shake the prison doors, and cause you to walk free (see Acts 16:16-34).
- Give Me glory that is due My great name, and watch Me come as the KING OF GLORY.
- Yes, lift up your voice in songs of worship, and the darkness will become light, the sorrow will turn to joy, the heavens will be open, and I will come with healing in My wings.
- Worship Me, and I will turn things around for you, give you victory upon victory, and cause your fiercest enemies to be utterly defeated.

FINAL THOUGHTS

No matter where you are in your battle, let me remind you that you come from a long line of overcomers. You are a mighty over-comer in the army of the Lord. May God give you the strength to fight on, peace in knowing the outcome, and refreshment from the joy of certain victory. Take heart and be encouraged, mighty overcomer. You are fighting on the winning side.

THE DRENCHED LIFE IS THE OVERCOMING LIFE. EVERY DAY, SEEK TO BE THOROUGHLY COVERED AND COMPLETELY FILLED WITH THE HOLY SPIRIT! LET THE HOLY SPIRIT LIVE BIG IN YOU!

The drenched life is the overcoming life. Every day, seek to be thoroughly covered and completely filled with the Holy Spirit! Let the Holy Spirit live BIG in You!

www.ingramcontent.com/pod-product-compliance
Lightning Source LLC
Chambersburg PA
CBHW070540090426
42735CB00013B/3032